Win

"There are two realities we face as Christians: we want to win for the kingdom, *and* we battle worry because of the sin-stained world we find ourselves in. Our thought lives can paralyze us from making progress and hold us back from all God desires for us. We are in a war for our minds, and Keri beautifully leads us to a better narrative in this book—one that will allow us to soar with our Overcomer. If you struggle with worry or anxious thoughts (let's be honest, we all do!), this is a must-read!"

— **Rebecca George,** author of *Do the Thing: Gospel-Centered Goals, Gumption, and Grace for the Go-Getter Girl*, and host of the *Radical Radiance* podcast

"What I do is determined by what I think, and what I think is determined by what I believe most deeply. Worry plagues the 'doing' and 'thinking' parts of our lives. But in this book, Keri invites us to search the depths of our own souls and examine what we truly believe at the core of who we are. The more my deepest beliefs are brought to light and reshaped by the gospel, the more worry begins to lose its power in my life."

— **Kyle Idleman,** best-selling author of *not a fan* and *One at a Time*

"If you are tired of feeling overwhelmed by your own thoughts that leave you paralyzed, Keri Eichberger is the friend and encourager you need to help you begin walking in victory. In *Win over Worry*, Keri graciously guides you to recognize how to unlearn unhealthy worry patterns and, more importantly, how to surrender and overcome them with the power of God and his Word."

— **Ashley Morgan Jackson,** author of *Tired of Trying*

"Friend, there's a rooted reason for all your worries, and God is the only way to permanently pull the worry roots from the garden of your heart. Confronting the evil stepsisters of worry and fear, Keri encourages you to open your heart to God and allow him to fill it where the root of worry once resided; to transform you from a worrier into a warrior. Choose today to set yourself up for victory over worry."

— **Wendy Pope,** best-selling author of *Wait and See: Finding Peace in God's Pauses and Plans*, Christian speaker, and Founder of Word Up Ministries

"Are you weighed down with worry? Keri Eichberger once was, but she's discovered how to overcome it and can show you how to overcome it too. This book is filled with hard-fought wisdom from a friend who has been there. She can empathize with your feelings and can guide you to conquer what has plagued you for too long. With authenticity and vulnerability, Keri can attest it is possible to *Win over Worry*—and can give you the practical steps to win as well."

—**Rachael Adams,** author of *A Little Goes a Long Way: 52 Days to a Significant Life*

"Worry seems to be invading the hearts of women in epidemic proportions—it is a battle many of us are fighting relentlessly. Keri Eichberger has breathed fresh life into a battle strategy that will help you to not only win over worry but also live a life of peace and hope. In her sweet yet moving literary style, Keri's answers are at once both rich and practical. If you, or a friend, have found yourself paralyzed by worry, *Win over Worry* will enable you to tackle the future with excitement rather than fear."

—**Carol McLeod,** Bible teacher, podcaster, and best-selling author

"What if you could have a real talk on worry with a good friend who really gets you? That's Keri. She offers affirmation of all your worries, plus gives you practical tips to handle them with God's help. You'll enjoy the creative and memorable ways she encourages you to choose joy and peace over worry and fear."

—**Sarah Geringer,** Christian blogger, speaker, podcaster, creative coach, and author of six books, including *Transforming Your Thought Life: Christian Meditation in Focus*

"In *Win over Worry*, Keri Eichberger gives us a go-to resource filled with practical and biblical help to stop the spiraling fear that paralyzes us. She helps us get to the root of our worry and turn it around with trusted truth. This is the message we need deep down to wrangle the unknowns and uncontrollables we face every day."

—**Lisa Appelo,** author of *Life Can Be Good Again: Putting Your World Back Together after It All Falls Apart*

WIN
OVER
WORRY

WIN
OVER
WORRY

Conquer What Shakes You and
Soar with the One Who Overcomes

KERI EICHBERGER

LEAFWOOD
PUBLISHERS
an imprint of Abilene Christian University Press

WIN OVER WORRY

Conquer What Shakes You and Soar with the One Who Overcomes

LEAFWOOD
P U B L I S H E R S
an imprint of Abilene Christian University Press

Copyright © 2023 by Keri Eichberger

ISBN 978-1-68426-242-7

Printed in the United States of America

Published in association with Blythe Daniel of The Blythe Daniel Agency, Inc., PO Box 64197, Colorado Springs, CO, 80962

Cataloging-in-Publication Data is on file at the Library of Congress, Washington, DC.

Cover design by Thinkpen Design, LLC | Interior text design by Sandy Armstrong, Strong Design

Leafwood Publishers is an imprint of Abilene Christian University Press
ACU Box 29138 | Abilene, Texas 79699

1-877-816-4455 | www.leafwoodpublishers.com

23 24 25 26 27 28 29 / 7 6 5 4 3 2 1

To Michael

The man who served his heart out to make
this dream of a calling come true.

CONTENTS

INTRODUCTION

HOPE FOR THE ANXIOUS WORRIER

Like the trickle of a leaky, faulty faucet. *Drip. Drip. Drip.*

Constant. Steady. And nagging.

Then progressing into a pestering flow. A stream of swelling water. That won't stop. Uncomfortably irritating.

Until it rushes, gushes, and bursts forth outside the confines of its intended space. Into a messy muck of madness.

It's your mind. Your consuming thoughts. Parading around constantly in your head. And your heart. Dripping, pulsating, throbbing.

Your complex circumstances, your unpleasing past, your uncertain future. Your decisions, your choices, overwhelming options. They're there. Always there. Pressing, cluttering, roaring.

Your people, your well-being, your everything. Distracting. Stressing. Pouring down. Incessantly filling your mind. More, more, more. And smothering.

It's worry.

And sometimes, too many times . . .

Fear.

I want to start here. I *feel* your pain.

You're anxious. Maybe scared. You feel defeated more days than you want to admit. Like the pressure will never let up. And it only seems to be getting worse. You wonder, *Have I always been this way? What in the world happened to me? Why me? Did God make me a worrier? I suppose. Maybe this battle in my brain is for my benefit somehow, someday. No clue how. But, it could be worse. I guess.*

You hate being on edge nonstop though. I know. I was you. Sometimes I still weather the same walk and fight the worry war. In fact, I've pretty much labeled myself an "anxious worrier" since before I can remember—always analyzing and anticipating the what-ifs of life, launching my stomach into backflips—fearful of and worried about everything. Well, maybe not everything, but it sure felt that way.

For one thing, I developed a major fear of flying. I mean it, major. I'm not talking Xanax and Benadryl material. No, more like a heavy-duty Valium to knock me out, or I was a raging heap of nerves. That is, if I could actually be coerced to get on the awful airplane. I worried about what would happen if . . . you name it.

For heaven's sake, I've been known to be fearful of fear itself. How ridiculous is that? As in, it's not so much that I've been afraid I'd die on that gargantuan flying machine. But wrecked at the mere thought of the anxious pain I'll suffer while my life flashes before me and the hundred-ton cylinder nosedives to the ground? Yep! Like, no joke, my lungs are tightening. I may lose my breakfast on the keys as I type.

And the dark? I'll never forget the sheer terror of being trapped in the pitch-black "Lilo and Stitch" ride in Disney World. I didn't release a bit of breath until the lights finally flipped back on. And no, I wasn't eight. Picture a wimpy thirty-five-year-old mom with three fearless kids sitting next to her. How embarrassing!

Can you relate to a word of this?

I'll tell you, worry certainly has a sneaky way of taking over before we even know it. Leaving us tied up tight, captive to its grip. And that was me.

Worry and fear.

The two seem to go hand in hand. Evil stepsisters or something. Where worry exists, *fear* is somewhere near her. At the surface, we may simply call our struggle "ruminating thinking" or "worry" before it escalates, hovering where the deceptive sister is hiding out. But make no mistake, she *(fear)* is there. Always. Worry and fear are synonymous. The manifested result of unresolved fear becomes worry. And likewise, a surplus of snowballing thoughts, what-ifs, and worries can blow up into paralyzing fear. Worry and fear.

Imagine sipping a single breakfast-blend cup of coffee as ground-level worry—it gets your thoughts (and body) moving. But upping your intake with a loaded double shot of espresso a day, year after year, will burst into full-blown, all-out, get-you-running *fear.* So, where do you measure up when it comes to small sums of worry or heaping doses of worry-driven fear?

How much of the craze do you think you're gulping down?

Do you even realize you're fearful? Or worrying? When you're overthinking yourself silly.

How about this. Can you remember when you *didn't* worry?

Maybe you've been consumed with an overload of this nonsense longer than you can remember. And it's dreadful. You know it. Downright depressing. Or on the flip side, you're blind to the repercussions of your worry. But the truth is, it's taking an enormous toll on you whether you know it or not.

Either way, here's the festering frustration. Deep within, you have an immense zest and zeal for life. You long for peace and clarity of mind, joy of heart, and rich significance and purpose. Don't you?

Yes. You're a dreamer. Wildly imaginative, wanting to see things, do things, and live the wonderful life God has planned for you. You want to use all your great gifts. You want to feel so alive. You believe down in the center of your soul that God can do anything through you, but you're limited by this crippling disease. Worry. It's holding you back.

The years are passing, flying faster and faster. And it appears that the more you experience life and the unavoidable devastation that comes with it, the more scared you get of stuff. More riddled with unease and uncertainty. Worry overtakes delight in life.

And it's no surprise. The concern and angst following our traumatic and tough experiences piled up, one on top of the other, until the intense mountain of weight became unbearable. You know this weight. Heavier with each year. Each pain. Each difficulty. Each responsibility.

Sadly, it seems relief comes only with your will to *avoid*, right? But even sadder, along with this common practice also comes avoiding a full life and all its grandiose potential blessings. Yet, that's all you know to do: notice fear; call yourself a worrier, overanalyzer, or overthinker; and determine to minimize the risk. Just avoid.

Oh, and this. How quickly we almost forget. You might ask God to help you cope. If the lofty, unsettling circumstance can't be avoided, guided coping is your only other desperate answer. Fortunately, you do know a God (or you soon will) who is well known to always be there to calm and ease your heart after the nagging attacks of your compounding ill-thinking. Maybe your soul is only softened partially when you glance his way. But hey, he didn't promise an easy life; he just promised to be by our side. Right? So, you're thankful for the Band-Aid, and you'll keep him in your back pocket simply for assistance. Because you're sure there's no way of escaping your anxious twitch. It's in you. You were born with it. After all, God made you this way. True of you?

But. No. God didn't. He didn't make any of us this way.

Anxiousness, unease, worry, fear. It doesn't come from God. Whatever we call our "crazy," it falls under our trust in the false way *we* see things (through filters of the world and the enemy), rather than our trust in the truth of the divinely beautiful way *God* orchestrated all things.

Here's the deal, I knew this. That God was my rock and the only truth. But for the longest time I still couldn't overcome.

Why?

Because, friend, you and I may have a greater predisposition to worry, anxiety, or fear than others, but we took on the majority of the chains we're shackled by. We *learned* these things. You applied this unfavorable pattern of thinking to yourself, or you allowed it in. I did.

And here's the better-than-good news. You can unlearn it. You truly can. I know this. I've lived this, fighting a war with worry most of my life. But I unlearned, and am still unlearning it now. And oh my goodness, how super frustrating that it took me forty-plus years to begin figuring it out. Forty stinking years. Let's believe you can start fighting the fight and unlearn faster than I did. And enjoy more of this lovely life you've been gifted. Listen, even if you're years beyond forty, I'm on fire to share with you that there is so much hope for you. I've tasted the richness and I know others who have too.

Oh, how much I want to help you dig deep and uncover, unlock, and understand your worry. And more importantly, I want to encourage you and see you through discovering the most indestructible armor and fear-resistant weapons purposed to crush this colossal battle. Equipping you to unlearn the worry that is so rudely snatching your smiles and your peace.

Yes, peace. Big-time worrier or not, I bet you're someone who craves peace even more than life itself sometimes. Me too. And you've probably felt deprived of this invaluable, yearned-for treasure. When you find peace, you feel one with God. And life tastes and smells so sweet. In the depths of your soul, I know you want that. And I am positively desperate for you to get there and stay there. Isn't that the key? To actually live locked in to God's lavish goodness, and not just visit every so often. You absolutely can.

We're going to shake off the layers and labels of a worrier and unleash the God-trusting warrior within. The identity our Maker gave us before the get-go. We're going to seek it, say it, eat it, repeat it, and most of all *live it* going forward. So we don't lose another second of our time spent soaked in the weariness of worry.

Essentially, we want to become warriors for our hearts, thoughts, and our abundantly blessed lives, rather than worriers of the mind. Are you with me?

What are you and so many of us worried about?

You're going to learn that with God, we really have *nothing* to worry about. Nothing. Together we'll own it, believe it, and once and for all live like worry is our past, not our present nor our future.

I'm with you, and so is he. Always has been, always will be. You'll see. Keep reading and you'll find the freedom you long for. Oh, sweet freedom. How? Together. You, me, and God. We're going to win over worry. We're going to conquer this nasty stealer of life. You are the King's mighty warrior, and the worrisome thoughts Satan has been slinging at you for too many years are approaching their final days.

If it's possible for me, it's absolutely possible for you. Be encouraged and set your vibrant hopes high. With your solidified faith in God's love, power, and trustworthy truths, your rocky road is getting ready to transform into more scenic, peace-filled, breathtaking views than you once imagined. Unleashing a fresh, new, fruitful life.

And I can't wait to ride along with you. All the way through. To the win.

Hands up! Here we go. :)

PART ONE

WORRIER

UNLEARN IT

ONE

UNDERSTAND IT
Where Your Battle Began

Does it really even matter how it started?

Your worry. Your tangled, temperamental, troublesome thinking. All that nonsense. It is what it is. Right?

And sure, I suppose it's true that trying to understand the nature of a problem is a big fat waste of precious time. If. If there's nothing you can do about it. But in the case of your "war with worry," you can most certainly do something.

It's possible you don't need much convincing that your worry is a problem, but you might need touches of persuading that it can be dismantled and resolved. It really can. Trust me. I've seen it. I've long-term lived it and am real-time living it. But I also know that, like anything that needs repair, you've first got to examine the dilemma in deeper depth to know exactly what to mend.

Our thoughts. They're complex, amen? And if your web of brain busters include *worry*, let's agree they need some straightening up and sorting through. I'm not singling you out, promise! Believe it or not, we all worry. All of us. I may have claimed to be a recovering worrier, but I'm really just implying my crazy head is a bit more under control than back when I was a big-league worrier. Yes, I certainly still worry.

Maybe you're similar. You can recall days of fighting the worry fight, but you're getting by okayish on most fronts. For now. Or maybe you're suffocating in a relentless disruption of fearful thoughts as you rummage through these very words.

But whether it's big doses of fear or slight, subtle concerns, worry will impact every soul who breathes. Which means this book is for you, for me, and even all the "perfect" persons who claim they aren't worriers.

That said, I'll take a stab and say that you do want to do something about worry. I'll go out on another limb and guess you even sense there's hope of change. Oh, yes, yes, yes. You are right on. And since it also seems we can agree we can't repair something if we have no clue what causes it, rewind with me, will you? Let's backpedal through some of the gusts and dust of life to understand how this battle began and where we went wrong, and get to winning over our worry.

Born Worriers

You know, it's stunning really. I've stumbled across a fascinating finding. My husband, Mike, and I have three-year-old twin girls. They came seven years after our third child, which currently equates to dealing with teen drama and potty training in the same blessed day. Woo-hoo! And, let me tell you, with five kids (one boy and four girls) I've navigated my fair share of child development, birth order, and externally influenced dynamics. But the enchanting phenomenon the twins convinced me of was that God absolutely assigned and handpicked some characteristics in the womb. Or well before.

I've literally witnessed two humans, born simultaneously, emerge with polar opposite personalities. Hannah Kate, the last to make her debut, is my sweet little test case for this subject. The girl wasn't six months old before she displayed that fear factor. I'm telling you, if it's possible for a three-year-old to be a worrier, she's one. Trembles at the top of the steps, holds her ears when the washing machine hits the spin cycle, and shudders with tears at the sight of an itsy-bitsy spider. God bless her!

Her twin sister has an opposite boldness and calm. Mallory was minutes old when I sensed that. I'll never forget the still demeanor and peaceful eyes of her five-pound frame lying next to me, keeping me composed, as the OB coaxed the timid Hannah Kate out into the world. It's been mesmerizing to watch their differences unveil ever since.

My point is, there is much we are born with. A huge gene pool of personality traits that God chose to mold us into the unique masterpieces he planned. But. There is much more to who we are, and who we will become, than our fickle, fleeting traits. Even if you inherited a specific struggle, you have huge hope of recovery. We all do. I don't believe God would allow any of his complete creations to keep a self-destructive trait without hope. In fact, he offers strength in all our weaknesses. If you've claimed the label of "worrier" since birth, meaning you think it's just who you are, I want to ignite a fire that you can be so much more. You were made to be so much more.

Worry Learned from Experience

Whether you were born with a bent to worry or not, I'm going to propose that's not where we park our main focus. Because, even if you showed up on day one as a Hannah Kate, the majority of worry we encounter is *learned*. Believe it or not, you can learn to worry as you begin to experience life. Yes, you can learn to be a worrier. Even if you were born as calm, collected, and bold as Mallory. What happens to us, and around us, combined with how we think, react, and then deal with the experiences, continues to develop our fear factor and worrier mindset. We learn worry. And more worry.

> The majority of worry we encounter is *learned.*

We may experience traumatic or seeds-of-worry-planting situations *personally*, *secondhand*, or merely through our *perception*, but all three affect us in profound ways. Ways that fuel fear and compound worrisome thoughts while we learn to cope, applying and acquiring unhealthy behaviors. Hang tight, though, because I'm going to walk you through *unlearning* by *retracing* your thoughts and experiences, and later *replacing* them with healthy truths, actions, and attitudes. (Hold this thought with me: Unlearning or relearning = Retracing and replacing.)

> Unlearning or relearning = Retracing and replacing.

Personal Experiences

The collective experiences we personally withstand have some serious potential to imprint the deepest scars on our thoughts and behaviors. Friend, what happened to you? Think back to your youngest hurt. Your first trauma. An early disappointment. Did you lose a close family member or cherished pet? Struggle with a move, suffer a shift in family dynamics, or trudge through a ridiculously rough school year? Think about it.

Secondhand Experiences

Living through the hurts and losses of the people around us can cut just as deeply as what we experience firsthand. When you were growing up, did you watch a friend's parents go through an ugly divorce, endure the loss of a child, lose their home, or suffer through an unfortunate accident? Think of others' pain.

Perceived Experiences

We don't have to be on the scene of our own or someone else's tragedy to form fearful thoughts and worry. A multitude of media outlets are relentless in trying to influence the way people think and perceive information. And too often, our translation of events is skewed and false, and leaves damaging defects. Was the news on nightly at the house of your youth? Maybe you caught peeks of a few too many movies that jaded you? Or overheard an excess of adult conversations, sending you to bed with vivid nightmares.

I bet you can rehash countless incidents from your past that may have stirred up "new to you" emotions and thoughts. They were all part of learning worry. As pricks, pains, and impressions nestle their way into your being, seeds of worry can be planted. When and how? Worry is born and bred when an underlying emotion from an experience is unguided and handed over to anything unreliable. Anything other than God. Before our faith has had the chance to ground us, we succumb to our immature reasoning and unreliable default defenses, learning (teaching ourselves) to cope, based on what we sense is necessity. So, if we don't know any better, then or now, when the hurts, dents, and imprints happen, that's pretty much when worry has fertile ground to grow.

> Worry is born and bred when an underlying emotion from an experience is unguided and handed over to anything unreliable. Anything other than God.

The Onset of Unhealthy Behaviors

What do you do when you experience pain, loss, and the blows of life? What habits do you default to? Do you see patterns? Any unhealthy ones? I suspect the answer is yes if you're reading these pages. And it makes perfect sense, since we soak in pain, loss, and suffering at such young ages no one could possibly expect us to reason maturely. Then, as soon as we repeat our initial coping strategies, they become nice and comfy, we default to them, and they become habits.

Surely you know the old saying, *old habits die hard*. Well, it's no wonder we carry on in our oblivious youth with limited, insufficient behaviors as we begin to plow through more adult stuff—the hard stuff. We've been doing it for years by now. It's what we know. It's easier to do what we know. And change? Change is hard. I've certainly learned some unsightly coping patterns myself—patterns common to all of us. *Anxious living, avoidance, and control.* Any of this sound familiar?

Maybe someone who's been around since your younger years has mentioned you've in fact always been a bit timid or displayed an anxious itch. But, if you're like me, you find it difficult to pinpoint with certainty exactly when you started to get wrapped up in unease. You basically landed yourself in a downward spiral of consuming concern or panic without a clue how you got there.

In gathering research for this book, I did some digging and soul searching, tracing back to my earliest memory of worry, which was only evident from panic attacks that showed up in high school. And now I can see clearly how it started.

The truth is, God was not my first line of defense in those days. I grew up in a Christian home with a mom and dad who loved each other and no doubt loved God. And I followed suit. Church was a huge part of my upbringing. Church choir, Sunday school, youth group, summer mission trips, and countless heartfelt vows to God of a life lived for him—yep! I played the part. "God girl," wholehearted.

That said, have you ever felt as if you knew all the things and were attempting to do all the things, yet your head couldn't convince your heart enough to convince your emotions, your impulses, and your automatic responses to react accordingly? That was me. I learned about and even declared God's love, power, and provision. But did my declarations affect my habitual worrisome thoughts and anxious behaviors? Not exactly.

Why is it so hard to take what we *say* we believe and convince our hearts to help us act in a like manner? Not acting out or living according to our stated beliefs is a sizable struggle for all of us, and probably a huge reason we have trouble changing and ridding our thoughts of all the distressing worry.

I eventually learned new lessons the long and harder way. But I did learn. And I changed. Rewind with me to my teen years and maybe you'll find yourself reflecting on your past too.

Seeds of Worry and Fear Planted

As teens have for generations, or at least where I'm from and back in the '90s, we spent most fall Friday nights at high school football games. Typically, only students of the two opposing schools and maybe their families would show up. So I was quick to notice a handful of boys among the crowd below the stands who looked out of place for the sell-out game with our rival.

The pride of our students stood strong. I'm speaking specifically of Jake, my back-then boyfriend. The misfit crew held my gaze as I created distance, catching a whiff of trouble. After all, they had just announced they were looking for a fight. Who wouldn't bolt?

But Jake hardly budged. His confident smiles grew to haughty chuckles, and the gang of boys took notice. Before I could process what was on the horizon, they were aggressively confronting him, and Jake's proud laughter turned to impulsive defense as a dozen heavy fists suddenly began swinging wildly at his face.

Within moments, I was handed a dangerous dose of fear, first-hand, through an experience that would plant toxic seeds of worry and leave a compounding impact on my thought life for years to come.

I bet you've experienced something that blindsided you with fear and etched seeds of worry in your soul. Maybe you wanted to run too, as I literally did.

I couldn't take any more. You can't take the *hard* you're some-times dealt either. Not alone anyway. And I didn't have to. You don't have to.

What do I mean by this?

Because God was there. God is *always* right there, even in the midst of danger. Problem was, I didn't run to him. Nope, I ran straight down the concession hallway, and I didn't stop until a friend who held it together enough to assess the scene confirmed all I cared about at that moment. That Jake was alive, and it was over. But that was only the beginning of seeds of fear establishing a stronghold in me.

> God is *always* right there, even in the midst of danger.

I didn't have a clue then how much this event would play a critical part in my worry life. What did surface is that I didn't have a lick of control over certain situations, and also that I could pos-sibly lose someone I genuinely cared for.

A hospital visit indicated that Jake was physically stable and well, but I can't say the same for the health of my heart and emotions. My focus was immediately directed toward the repercussions for him. I mean, he was the real victim, you know? But what exactly was happening to me as I looked at my own pain? I'll tell you what. One of those nasty seeds of worry was planted. Because I didn't off-the-bat hand over my pain to God, the only one who can make good of it, I paid the consequences and learned to live with a little more nagging worry.

Anxious Living

But life goes on. A point comes after any struggle, trauma, or painful event when life must move on. Though we wish fiercely we could push pause and avoid getting near anything or anyone that reminds us of the dreaded occurrence, we quickly learn that we often aren't able to completely separate ourselves from the pains of the past. Or the fears of the future. That is, if we want a semi-normal life again.

So, what do we do? I know what I did, and my guess is you've done something similar. We reenter life with our will set to "self-protect," tightly clenching our sidekick "anxiety."

You better believe I avoided football games like the plague for the rest of that season, and any large crowd, for that matter. Until a time came the next spring when my whole crew was gearing up for a local Memorial Day festival.

Riddled with worry, I finally convinced myself it was safe enough and about time I got out in the real world again. But, no surprise, it wasn't long before the mass of people overwhelmed my senses. The unsettled anxiety that came not long before was gnawing at my instinct to exit. I was learning that colossal congregations would trigger and stir up anxious seeds of self-protection. Because here's what happens when we don't properly dissolve those nervy grains. The toxic seeds swell so uncomfortably that we begin to despise the very events that we used to love and thrive on.

Anxiety to Panic

I began to experience my first panic attack leaving the festival. At first, I became dizzy, disoriented, and weak. By the time I made my way to the driveway of my parents' house, well before curfew, I refused to get out of the car. I was too scared.

If you've endured a panic attack, maybe you know this, but if not, the best I can describe it is like entering another dimension. One that's foggy, fragile, and totally surreal. I wasn't right. And I was positive if I got out of the car, someone would *get* me. Who that would be and what they would do, I had no clue! But I was paralyzed with fear and certain danger was pounding on my door.

Before I could pull myself out of the victim's seat, I was off to the hospital with Mom and Dad to see what was up with their loopy daughter.

When the blood work results returned with only slightly low potassium levels, the doctor handed me a banana and sent me on my way, nonchalantly reporting I may have experienced a panic or anxiety attack.

That sounds pretty basic. Truthfully, I was too young to have much of a care. By the time we were headed home, all I knew was that I was good and sleepy, feeling safe for the time being, and interested in resuming a fairly normal life—void of problems. But also void of plans to attend another big festival or crowded event, that's for sure.

Red Flags of Avoidance and Control

Now, one might assume that after this blip of hardship, a red flag would've appeared, screaming, "Keri, are you okay? There seems to be something going on with you (ahem, hospital visit), and if you don't get a handle on it, how do you expect to enjoy life?" But I was a teenager, for heaven's sake. Yes, I might have been among the majority of sixteen-year-olds who were convinced they had their life figured out. But not only was I wrong then, we would all be wrong making that claim today.

> **There's always so much more God wants to teach us.**

There's always so much more God wants to teach us. I know this now, but then I definitely didn't connect the dots enough to see unhealthy anxious patterns brewing.

How about you? Have you muddled through painful experiences that have manifested unhealthy patterns of anxious living in you?

I'll tell you where the anxious living led me. Straight into the arms of avoidance and numbing distractions. Quick fixes allowing me to "function" in environments I once enjoyed, but that had become too difficult to manage on my own. That's what I think most of us do. We attempt control by numbing and avoiding so we can *function* in our *dysfunction*. This is difficult to admit (putting on my humble hat here), but though I was still a very cautious aim-to-please kind of teen, if I wasn't avoiding an event altogether, I rarely attended another football game, school dance, or social affair without the liquid courage of a few drinks.

> **God never intended *anything* but him to completely fulfill us.**

For the record, bad idea! Bad, bad, don't-do-what-I-did idea. But I honestly didn't see the harm. Then. What I did notice was that all of a sudden, I was enjoying a little more of the things I once loved, and I could escape some of my pain at the same time. Numb and distract. And life seemed more tolerable and fun. Temporarily.

News flash! God never intended *anything* but him to completely fulfill us. Not the boy that I thought was my entire existence, not a drink that takes the edge off, not the things we buy that boost happiness until the newness fades. The avoiding, the numbing, and the pursuit of control will eventually fail to fulfill. Always.

The sad truth is, the years between the beginning of my quest to numb worry and my breaking point postcollege were indisputably the darkest years of my life. Oh, what I would give to have recognized all along that God wanted nothing more than to fill every empty space with his fullness.

Accelerated Anxiety

Leading up to this breaking point, my numbing measures finally failed to be strong enough to fight off a return of panic. My approaches were not solutions, they were Band-Aids. And sure enough, panic came screeching back full force in 2001. Specifically, September 11th.

Paralyzing fear struck the country that day. It wasn't long before my anxiety that, again, had never been handed to God, would snowball back into a panic attack that would consume me for days.

The Mayo Clinic describes symptoms of panic attack (among others) as "Dizziness, lightheadedness or faintness. Numbness or tingling sensation. Feeling of unreality or detachment."[1] I had all of that. For three full days. I'm not sure what it was all about—the purpose of that nasty nightmare, I mean. But I think God has a creative way of allowing things in our life, which may not be something we'd ever desire, to wake us up a bit.

> God wants to be so much more than our backup plan.

[1]"Panic attacks and panic disorder," MayoClinic.org, May 4, 2018, https://www.mayoclinic.org/diseases-conditions/panic-attacks/symptoms-causes/syc-20376021.

Remember, I was a "God girl." I knew all the things and loved all the things about him. Problem was, I wasn't living like it when life handed me the big stuff. I'd been living anxiously, ultimately relying on myself, and keeping God in my back pocket like a friend you take along for the ride instead of one who can, and wants to, carry all your *stuff* for you. And God wants to be so much more than our backup plan.

The Beginning of Unlearning

With a heart desperate for healing, I did start to wake up. I found my way back to church in my final year of college, marking the beginning of unlearning the unhealthy habits I had relied on for far too long. I sought medical attention for the not-so-fabulous way my body seemed to be weathering the storms. Okay, maybe my mom pleaded for me to get help. Goodness! My poor parents.

Please never underestimate the need for medical advice if you struggle with anxiety or panic attacks. But I will proudly tell you, there is so much more beyond medicine. I was, not to my surprise, prescribed a few meds by a psychiatrist. But for me, the side effects I experienced weren't worth the little help I got. This won't be everyone's story, but in my case, and maybe others, God wanted to alter my heart more than my body with only medication or temporary fixes.

> God wanted to alter my heart more than my body.

I needed the deeper work in my heart. Actually, we all need that. God was pressing, and pressing some more, to get my attention for years, but I was too self-focused and numb to hear him. Man, I wish I had been more awake. He had such fantastic plans for me. And I know for a fact he wants to grab *your* attention too. You may be sleepwalking through life right now as I was. But I am sure of this. He has great plans for each of us, but generally we're too stubborn, settled in our own toxic thoughts, seeking our own way, to see his better way.

You Have a Choice to Unlearn and Change

Worry is all in our thoughts. Jennie Allen shares in her book *Get Out of Your Head* how interrupting our thoughts, which follow our emotions, with the simple statement "I have a choice," can change everything.[2] Friend, I hope you hear this and don't dismiss it. This simple, interrupting thought can change your thought patterns as well as your "worry life." You have a choice.

You absolutely do have a choice when it comes to your thought life. And you most certainly do have a choice when it comes to your worry. You have a choice over how you respond to circumstances and over what you use to fill a void. But we cannot go it alone. If you do, you will fail. You just will. I don't say that to be harsh. I say it to relieve you of the intense pressure of flying solo, and to give you hope that you will have all the help you need.

> God is your helper, with all the right weapons to fight for you.

I am here, for one. I've been there. I'm still there many days. But now I'm on a mission to divulge all I've learned, with God's help, in changing my thinking, smashing the nagging worries, learning healthy responses, and freeing myself from paralyzing fears. But hear this—I'm just the messenger. God is your helper, with all the right weapons to fight for you. It's time to lock arms with him in a new battle plan!

[2] Jennie Allen, *Get Out of Your Head: Stopping the Spiral of Toxic Thoughts* (Colorado Springs: Waterbrook, 2020), 40.

Worry Compounds When Repeated

You may know that God is next to you at all times, believe he can fight your battles, and trust that he can be trusted. But, maybe like me you've been thinking thoughts and living behaviors that indicate otherwise. You've been practicing worry and learning to become a bigger worrier. Fearful thoughts have run so rampant that faulty thoughts became more natural and more comfortable than the truth. Even God's truth.

This is the way it spirals. One worry leads to another, which leads to another.

Scientifically speaking, in Henry Emmons's book *The Chemistry of Calm*, he writes, "Many of us strengthen *unhealthy* nerve circuits through repetitive practice. Every time we repeat a fearful or defeatist thought, we strengthen the connections that make it easier to have that thought again."[3]

When it comes to unaddressed worry, or worry addressed with faulty coping, we can sabotage ourselves with habitual thoughts one worry and fear at a time. But you probably didn't realize you were self-destructing, or recognize that you could be learning fulfilling ways to satisfy the empty gaps in your mind. You do not have to continue spiraling downhill without a productively practical way to combat the worry. Let's look at how we start!

God Fills the Empty Spaces

The good news is, God perseveres in pursuing our attention. And we can wake up at any point in this battle, unlearn, and overcome. We are constantly capable of opening up and allowing God to richly fill the hollow spaces in our hearts that lead to fear.

---

[3] Henry Emmons, *The Chemistry of Calm: A Powerful, Drug-Free Plan to Quiet Your Fears and Overcome Your Anxiety* (New York City: Touchstone, 2010), 234.

Spaces we clog up with everything else, leaving us sadly lacking results.

What do you fill your empty spaces with? Social media, bingeing with Ben & Jerry's or Netflix, unhealthy relationships, obsessive housework, excess spending, complaining and gossip?

Maybe God wants to fill all your empty spaces and sunken soul. What do you think? I say yes. Psalm 107:9 affirms, "For he satisfies the longing soul, and the hungry soul he fills with good things" (ESV).

He satisfies.

He fills.

So why is it that we seek healing and relief everywhere else before we seek it from God? Why do we strive to fill the empty hollows of our hearts with everything other than him?

Friend, God does want to fill those places. Desperately.

Can you consider with me that much of the worry and anxious striving you live with stems from how you've learned to deal with the disappointments or pain you've experienced? Habits that don't resemble a heart fully surrendered to God filling the gaping holes?

Can you consider that if you chose the perfectly capable Lord to fill those spaces, the canvas of your life would be that much more joyful, peaceful, and better?

Does it even seem possible to change? Oh, it absolutely is possible. Remember, we absolutely do have a choice.

You Can Choose to Overcome

Trouble is, if you're like me, you've tried to overcome before. Given up at times. Lost hope. And though you're desperate to get a grip and live a luscious life free from worry, you're certain based on worry's escalation that God must have just *made* you this way for a reason.

So, what do you do now?

You make the choice to change. You make a choice to fill the gaps with God.

Because, I'll repeat, God did not make you a worrier. God is not the author of anxiety, and he is not the one who instilled fear into your life. That would be Satan. God is the fear conqueror, not the fear creator. He can conquer your fear and win over all your worries.

> **God is the fear conqueror, not the fear creator.**

You may be predisposed to anxiety. I am. And that might mean we have to dig a little deeper and roam a road to recovery a little longer. But even you and I can choose thoughts and behaviors that lead away from worry and toward peace.

If only I'd initiated infusing God into the voids of life thirty years ago. And, oh to be able to speak these lessons learned to my former self and live a redo with a touch more of his ease. But I cannot sit in regret here, because I surely wouldn't be surrounded by my treasured blessings of today without my past wins and losses. And likewise for you! But, from this day forward . . . I choose to bring God in first.

Will you make the choice with me? Choose to bring God in.

> But seek first his kingdom and his righteousness, and all these things will be given to you as well. (Matt. 6:33)

Seek him first. This is the magical master key to unlock the peace you've been famished for. You can choose to seek him. You can choose to direct your thoughts and worries. And the final half of that scripture, "and all these things will be given to you," means if you seek him first, you will indeed be blessed. Sounds fantastic, right?

> **Life is just so much sweeter when we choose him.**

Instead of anxious striving, let's start striving to first fill our hollow hearts, our vacant voids, our mangled moments, displeased desires, and empty existence with his Word, his love, his peace, and all of his amazing goodness. Life is just so much sweeter when we choose him.

God Is the Ultimate Solution

We've been learning from the lens of the enemy's twisted perspective, and then spitting out worrisome thoughts and destructive behaviors that lead us away from God's will, and it just doesn't work.

But, just as we've learned and practiced our worries from our past experiences, we can unlearn a life of unhealthy thinking with God's help. In the chapters ahead, we'll replace the old, unreliable, unfavorable thoughts and behaviors with the lasting solutions of God's truths and promises as we dive deeper and deeper to the root of our worries and fears. More importantly, we'll journey together to overcome, discovering practices to bust down the old ways and shape and mark new habits.

Whatever it is that worries you, God is the solution to change those thoughts. He offers all the armor, every shield and weapon to fight this war and win it. All it takes from you right now is a choice. An open heart to God's openhanded help and a willingness to change are the first steps forward in winning this war.

Will you accept that you do have a choice and that you can change? It's not so much about what you can do; it's about what God can do. And in case you need the reminder, he can absolutely do all things.

It's time to swim out and sink your feet into the sand. We may walk through water deeper than our comfort zone. But in doing this, we'll once and for all dig up and destroy what is buried at the bottom of our worry.

Be encouraged! Gradually your heart can believe the new thoughts you'll minister to your mind. You will rise reinforced with great peace in the unshakable truth that we have nothing to fear with our God who defeats it. Together we'll step out shielded with armor. And you will stand sturdy and secure. Safeguarded with the hope of conquering the paralyzing worry and fear that have plagued you.

> **We have nothing to *fear* with our God who defeats it.**

Accept God as your rock-solid shield, and let's keep fighting!

REFLECTION QUESTIONS

1. Can you recall past experiences, personal, secondhand, or perceived, that you handled in ways that may have planted seeds of worry?

2. Do you practice anxious living, avoidance, or numbing? Any other potentially unhealthy habits that you use to cope with past trauma or pain?

3. How can you allow God to fill the gaps instead of suppressing worry with numbing distractions?

4. Do you believe you have a choice to change? Do you believe God can help you? How?

TWO

UNRAVEL IT
Identifying Your Every Worry

What do you *think* about?

Right now, you're thinking, *What kind of question is this?* Everything and anything, right? Hand raised, that's me.

You know, I've heard it's actually possible for men to "not think," and I'm sorry, but I just can't buy it. Even when I try to think about nothing, I'd have to admit I'm thinking, "I'm trying to think about nothing." And then as quickly as I get bored with this notion, my mind warp-speed skips to the most recent rumination of thoughts about, I don't know . . .

- *What to prepare for dinner tonight and who's going to hate it.*
- *Why my son didn't get more playing time in the ball game last night.*
- *How in the world my sister always has so much more energy than me.*

- *Is this sliver of cake and scoop of ice cream going to make me feel bloated tomorrow morning?*
- *Oops, I forgot to send a note to school for my daughter to be a car rider today.*
- *Does (insert name) like me? Why doesn't she like me?*
- *Man, will we ever have enough money to take the kids back to Disney?*
- *I wonder what I can invent or invest in to put some extra cash in the bank, allowing a smidge more fun and freedom in this worn-down life.*

Think. Think. Think. (Can't help but picture Winnie the Pooh here.)

Maybe you are part of this so-called breed that can blank-pause the brain briefly. Even so, we *all* have thoughts that consume us. The only varying factor is what we focus our thoughts on.

But wait a minute, we're talking about *worry*. So, why didn't I ask what you worry about?

Here's what I believe. There are some out-to-lunch souls out there, maybe you, who honestly don't think they are worriers. They are thinkers, of course. But worry? That sounds a little harsh and not so relatable to how they process their inner workings.

Well, I've got a slice of humble pie to serve up here. We agreed in the last chapter we can't repair something when we don't know the cause of the problem. But I'd say the more obvious consensus could be that we can't repair something we don't even know *exists*. Meaning, until you call out your faulty thoughts for the reality of the no good they actually are, you'll go on permitting your mind to think itself crazy. If you say you're not worried but can rattle off consuming thoughts that stir you up or melt your mojo, worry is written all over your thought life and you don't even know it.

I know I've been hashing out worry as if this book was written for you. But there's a slim chance you're just doing someone a favor by entertaining their suggestion to delve into this message. You're positive you've got loads of junk to dismantle, but worry isn't your downfall. Now, a book titled *How about Happy, Ditching Discouragement, Tackling Trust Issues, Pursuing Purpose, Nixing Negativity,* or *Fighting Back at Frustration* might appeal to your latest battle. But maybe you're not so much a worrier, true?

The Wrong Lens

Let me ask you another question. Have you ever had one of those issues (see my list of clever titles) and tried to clean it up with no lasting luck? If so, you might be trying to wipe clean the wrong lens. And this suggestion may make more sense when I tell you a super sweet toddler story.

My Hannah Kate, who is four now, loves to slip her curious fingers into all my personal spaces. She must fantasy-envision undiscovered vaults of hidden gems in the master bathroom cabinets. I can no longer even apply makeup without her dabbling in the blush palette to emulate her mom's delicate attempt to brush up the weathering years. And her second favorite spot to investigate— my writing desk drawer. It's like a treasure chest to her fascinated innocence. It holds the catchall of forbidden tiny odds and ends sure to enchant any childlike curiosity.

During the early morning escape of my quiet time resting in my desk swivel chair, I believe she's come to recognize when I'm engrossed in daily devotions and oblivious to movement and sounds outside my invisible bubble. That became apparent to me last week when the drawer slid open a few inches and an old pair of my prescription glasses emerged, landing crookedly on her scrunched-up little face. I hardly noticed until she proudly shouted, "Mom, look at me!" My attention was captured by this picture-worthy cuteness, like many moments with spontaneous toddler interactions. But then her smile turned sideways and began to fizzle as a confused look brought her next request. "Can you wipe these off? I think they aren't clean. I can't see very well."

Problem was, they were as speck-free as they were the last time I desmudged and microfiber-cleaned them. I could perfectly polish the lenses again and again, but the fact is, she still wouldn't be able to see. That is, not until she was looking through the right lenses. Or in her case until she took the lenses off.

It occurred to me that, like Hannah Kate, we sometimes look through the wrong lens when analyzing our thoughts. We peer through a false or faulty filter, not 100 percent sure what we're truly looking at. We attempt to fix what *looks* wrong or seems skewed, only to find ourselves simmering on the same struggles. Sometimes we call our annoying thoughts *overthinking, stress, negativity,* or *frustration,* when if we took the glasses off or switched to a new set of spectacles, we might gain clearer vision and find webs of worry that need sorting through on a deeper level.

Worry vs. Thoughts

In all our humanness, most of the things we think about, we also worry about. As in, any thought we ponder that causes the slightest strife, we can go ahead and call *worry.* But regardless of what you want to label the thoughts that run wild between your ears, if you're interested in getting a handle on your thought life and taming these rugged runways, keep working through this chapter with me.

But seriously, why does it even matter what we call these little brain entertainers anyway? Worry or just *thoughts.* Worrying or plain *thinking.* I'll tell you why it matters to me. *It matters to God.* And I'm not making this up. The Bible doesn't say not to think. But it does say not to *worry.* Over and over again. And then again. So personally, if I catch a clue that I have some worrying going on in my thinking, I'd love to know this, so I can kick it out for the sake of living my best life (we all want large doses of that) according to the only foolproof trusted life manual on God's good green earth.

> **The more we can dump out and stare at the gunk and junk, the better we can properly place the clutter and set up the win.**

Okay, so maybe you don't need convincing that your thoughts are riddled with worry, but I have a hunch both of us sit in denial regarding the absolute full extent that worry warps our minds and sabotages what may have started as simple "innocent" pondering. Whichever end of the spectrum you find yourself on—aware of a handful of worries or picking up unease out of every fragmented speculation that pops up—we agreed we need to see it (all of it) to unravel it. The more we can dump out and stare at the gunk and junk, the better we can properly place the clutter and set up the win.

Getting Honest

I grappled with some restless thoughts just last Sunday morning. The nature of a household of five kids, mom and dad working remotely, and a forgotten dog lends itself to crazy-train parents, ruthlessly forcing intertwining schedules to fit into the waking hours allotted for each day. That's putting it mildly. *Breathe . . .*

Nonetheless, I have a relentless God-given desire to connect deeply with my husband. *God bless him.*

After speed showering before church this blessed Sabbath, I paused—disappointed, unsettled, and frustrated with my husband's recent distractedness. Can't imagine why. I plopped down on the edge of the bathtub (my only alone moments most days), and as is common in my discouragement, I called on *Jesus,* my lifeline. *What's going on? Is it him? Maybe it's me? God, what is it???*

(Me innocently thinking. Okay, with maybe a little worry strewn in there.)

And then a song breezed through my inner ear almost audibly. It was as familiar as the days I'd rehearsed it as a church-choir youth in maybe the seventh grade . . . "Search me, O God, and know me, try me and know my heart. . . . See if there be any wicked way in me, and lead me in the way everlasting."[1] I think it's so sweet how God whispers words we need when we call on him. Songs, verses, phrases of wisdom, what have you, our good counselor is perfectly creative and tender in our vulnerable moments of humility. I felt he was telling me to take a deeper look into my own heart, my anxious thoughts, and my actions—not my husband's. The only ones I have control over. Yep, I can't (nor do I want to) control my husband. I left for church in a touch more silence as I held onto the "see if there be . . . in me" part.

> God whispers words we need when we call on him.

Search Your Thoughts

That's what I want you to do with me. Let's search our hearts and minds with God and see what's there that he's saying "let's not." Where's the worry? We need to can it. So let's stir it all up and pour it out to look a little closer.

By the way, in case you didn't notice, the song the Lord sent me follows Scripture, like many old hymns and even contemporary masterpieces. Psalm 139, verses 23 and 24 read . . .

> Search me, God, and know my heart; test me and know
> my anxious thoughts. See if there is any offensive way in
> me, and lead me in the way everlasting.

---

[1] Allen Pote, "Psalm 139" (Dallas, TX: Choristers Guild, 1992).

Ironically, the church sermon that morning transitioned almost seamlessly from my swirling manifestation of contemplations. Well, maybe not so ironically. I know better. There are no coincidences with God. If you shout out to him for some aid and assistance, you better believe what's coming from all angles will have implications based on your request that he wants to speak straight to your heart through. So, if you cry out, I'd suggest you perk up those ears and be ready for what pops up.

In my case, Kyle Idleman, senior pastor of our church, came at me full throttle with "Blind Spots: Uncovering the Hidden Emotions That Sneak Up on You." Our new sermon series. Okay, okay, I know, I asked for it. Search me, test me, show me what I can't see, what I'm *blind* to. Oh boy, there's so much. We see most of the world through the lens of what others are doing wrong and we're dang good at holding one hand over an eye at our own offenses.

I'm sad . . . It's his fault.

I'm not worried . . . I'm just planning for the future.

I'm not scared . . . I'm being responsible.

If you'll humble yourself, slow down, and ask God to help you explore the depth of your own heart and thoughts, you'll find flaws. You'll find lots of worry, and then fear.

Dump It Out

You ready to lay it all out there with me? Whether you're sure of your every last worry and ready to burn each blasted frustration in the fire. Or you're just beginning to buy into the idea that you worry more than you realize (in which case you're only on the verge of tinkering with the potential of leveling out some of the uneasy thoughts and stirrings driving you a little nuts and hindering your happy). Either way, we've got to break through to the bottom of this, and I'd love the honor of working through a brain dump with you.

Here is what we're going to do with it: determine what we're really and truly worried about. *Why?* For the sake of finding fears buried under the sludge of the mud, to raise them up into the light of clarity, and demolish them. The light and power of God that can infuse all the good stuff that crumbles and crushes all that nasty apprehension, uncertainty, and turbulence of fear. YES!

I'll go first. And maybe you can borrow a few of mine and work side by side with your own worries. But if you have others, or we walk in different worlds, so to speak, you'll get the drift and can off-load yours by my example.

Okay, here I go, drawing a big brain bubble, and dumping all the general thoughts that surface and take up any space at all in my thought life on a given day. Scope out my best shot at it:

Making friends • Purpose •
Politics • Connection with spouse •
A strained relationship • Being on time •
Kids' health • Paying bills • Covering college tuition •
Retirement • People pleasing • Kids' sports • Losing weight •
Getting in shape • Losing a loved one • Kids' safety • Getting
enough rest • Husband's happiness • My kids' happiness •
My happiness • An injury • An illness • An upcoming
doctor's appointment • Work • Deadlines • War •
Travel plans • Finding love • Serving

Clearly I need a much bigger bubble. And this is a simply a snapshot of some of the hard-to-admit thoughts that hang over my head day in and day out. There are hundreds more itty-bitties, maybe related to many of these, that could make an appearance above if I spent more time sifting through my personal cloud of boiling sentiments.

Can you relate to any thoughts on my list? Go ahead and add yours. Glaring at mine, it's apparent that this fluster I'm filling thought space with is loaded with excessive worry. Take a look at each one. See if you can detect it. Imagine how worry might wiggle its way into each concept.

Connecting with my spouse?
We're better than some. He loves me. But does he really get me? Will we ever be in sync?
Busted! . . . Worry!

Retirement?
Let's be honest, you may think about it with excitement for 2.5 seconds, but I bet you make your way to wonder if you'll have enough money, energy, companionship . . .
Yep, worry again!

My kids' happiness?
Even if all's okay for now (never completely), in a matter of moments you slip into "but when's the shoe going to drop?"
There it is . . .
Worry!

Covering college?
We have some time. It's super expensive, but God will provide. I don't see how though! . . .
And more worry!

Fear under Worry. Ask "WHY?"

Now that we've poured out all our vulnerable thoughts and are starting to pick up on the worry that's present, we can travel on to the next level of investigation and see if there's some unresolved fear causing the brunt of your consuming musings and stresses. And I'll settle with you right now why that's a big deal. Where there's fear, there is darkness taking hold of you, or it will if you don't point a finger at it, snatch it from your blind spots, and kick it quick. And the truth of the matter is, if there's worry, there's also fear. It's there, under your every worry. And that's what we're really after. So don't walk away now.

> Where there's fear, there is darkness taking hold of you, or it will if you don't point a finger at it, snatch it from your blind spots, and kick it quick.

You've called to your own attention what you worry about, and now it's time to understand what you truly fear. By asking *why, why,* and *why* some more. Just like an inquiring toddler persistently posing this three-letter word to make sense of the mystery before her, so are we to unveil the unknown fear smothered in worry.

I'll pick one that I began to crack open, and then you can venture on your own scavenger hunt with your worries. So, I'm worried about covering college tuition (based on the fact that I think about it in a not-so-settling manner most of the time). But what am I *really* worried about? *Why* am I worried about that? *Why?*

Yes, there's surely a reason. There's a rooted reason for all your worries, right? We can't always just stop it. *I'm worried about covering the cost of college for my FIVE kids, and the thought is no fun, so I'm just going to stop it.* No, not so simple. There's a reason. It goes much deeper than my kids' ability to go to college or not. Simply suggesting I just *stop it* will allow me, at best, to temporarily move on to another stewing thought, or worse, force me to bury the worry deeper in the dark where fear finds gasoline to fuel the fire.

So, then *WHY*? (And keep asking *why* until you've nailed something!)

> *WHY am I worried about how to cover college expenses?*
> Because . . . if I can't afford it, I'll have to borrow money.
>
> *WHY am I worried about borrowing immense amounts of money?*
> Because . . . I'll be in debt forever.
>
> *WHY am I worried about having long-term debt?*
> Because . . . we'll have to work until we're ninety and never be able to retire.
>
> *WHY am I worried about a delayed retirement?*
> Because . . . this body is aging fast, and I won't be able to enjoy the fullness of life I've dreamed of before the good Lord calls me home!

Sounds like a form of FOMO to me. Fear of missing out on the good life. *Sheesh!* Side note: I hope all my worries don't surface so selfishly. I thought this was about my kids! Ouch!

But now that we're staring at the root FOMO on my future, you see how telling me to stop ruminating on the cost of college isn't addressing the real issue at all. It's like telling me to wipe off the glasses I'm wearing that are the wrong prescription and just *see*. I can try the quick-fix suggestions, but the resolution will remain foggy. And likewise, until I adjust filters to lenses made to see worry clearly and ask *why*, *why*, and *why*, I won't find a root fear. Can't see it! And only when we see it can we attack it.

You might get the picture here, but maybe you should jot down one of your worrisome thoughts, call it worry, and see what fears you come up with after asking *why* until you land on a familiar fear. For example, I arrived at these common fears from a few worries I noted. Worry about my kids' safety boiling down to . . . *Fear of losing a child.* Worry about making friends . . . *Fear of rejection.* Worry about meeting deadlines . . . *Fear of failure.* You know these fears, don't you? All too well, huh?

Bring It to the Light

What's happening here? We've gone rummaging through our closets stuffed full of thoughts and worries, and now we're loaded down by some pretty bulky fears with piercing eyes scowling up at us. They are exposed. And that in itself feels kind of dreadful, scary, and heavy. But here's the good news. As much as the world wants to gloss over the weighty dark stuff you're busy digging up, this is exactly where we need it to dissolve the darkness. In the light.

> But everything exposed by the light becomes visible—and everything that is illuminated becomes a light. This is why it is said: "Wake up, sleeper, rise from the dead, and Christ will shine on you." (Eph. 5:13–14)

Do you see it? The Bible is encouraging us to uncover what is hidden, allowing it to become visible, thus giving it the opportunity to become a "light." Meaning what? We must give "the bad" the chance to make something *good*, as God shines and slathers his blessings, goodness, and abundance all over it. An ashes-to-beauty transformation happens when we dig up our worry. Sounds pretty fantastic, amen? Unearthing our worry from the dirt and welding it into the longed-for luscious colors in the flower garden of our vibrantly planned life. You'll see this more in action as we keep dissecting and fighting our fears in chapters to come, but hold on to this. Spill it out and see it for what it is, and you will be on your way to the win.

> An ashes-to-beauty transformation
> happens when we dig up our worry.

Staying Stuck in the Dark

There's one big problem though. Life doesn't lend itself to exposing our darkness. This is the key point Pastor Kyle was highlighting on that coincidental sermon series that smacked me in the face. We stay stuck, stumbling along and not checking our blind spots or assessing our thought life. And what keeps us stuck? We are distracted, we are the dirty "B" word—busy—and we are addicted. To eardrum-bursting loud, get-me-from-here-to-there-in-Mach-speed pace, and I-can't-get-enough-stuff-exploding-at-the-seams engorgement. And all this "stuck stuff" is wickedly disruptive of God's serenity, working like a best-selling 1000 SPF light blocker.

We're the problem. We stay stuck in the darkness, oblivious to the depth of our inner turmoil, because we don't slow down enough to set down the foggy glasses, rub the sleep out of curious eyes, and wide-eye focus on what's swirling fast inside us. In fact, I'll venture to say if you whipped through my bubbled-up thoughts without considering your own, you need to wave a red flag, take a hard pause, and prod and probe for your potential blind spots. Oh, and if you do simmer down and you still struggle to unravel any darkness, check for pride. It gets the best of me too. When you are busy pointing your finger at the person closest to you as the basis of your frustrations and fears, snatch that red flag again and redirect your aim exactly 180 degrees. Sting!

What keeps us from checking our blind spots? Buying into the beat of the world's rhythm and running modern culture's rat race distracts us from truth and light. We're the problem. The world is the problem. We've got to search our souls, sway slower, breathe deeper breaths, keep our lenses clear, and ensure we're exposing ourselves to the true light and looking through the proper filter, again and again and again.

> **Buying into the beat of the world's rhythm and running modern culture's rat race distracts us from truth and light.**

Clearing the View with the Lens of Light

The things that keep us stuck, looking through the wrong lens, or fogging up our filters, are the complete opposite of what envelops us in the light of the pure truth.

So, what is this right lens? It's the truth nestled and swelling in our centers. It's the lens of truth. The lens of light. The light of God's truths.

Let me ask you, what truths of God do you know? What lens of truth can you apply and determine to keep peering through? Here's what I know. God is light. God is love. God is peace. God is comfort. He is always the light in darkness. The light of life. I know when I seek him, I find him, and find light. Looking to and through God is the key to finding the light. And the light makes our fear fizzle out. So, we stay unstuck, seeking and revealing our worries and rooted fears to the light, by continuing to focus through the lens of his truths. Thus, we enable our thoughts and cloudiness to indulge in the encompassing brilliance of his compassion, comforts, and blessings. The light. His light.

> Looking to and through God is the key to finding the light. And the light makes our fear fizzle out.

A mint-green sticky note is perched on the wall above and behind my computer screen with the handwritten words "Return Your Eyes to Me." I wrote this note to self on a day the shadows fell hard on me. It is an invitation to you as well. When the chaos and confusion of thoughts start swelling and the darkness sweeps over you like a dense storm cloud, face your fears, adjust your focus, put on his lens, and return your eyes to the light. To him.

> When Jesus spoke again to the people, he said, "I am the light of the world. Whoever follows me will never walk in darkness, but will have the light of life." (John 8:12)

This is powerful. Out of the darkness, we can have the light of life. Wow!

I hope you're encouraged. And I hope you now know that you aren't alone. The whole wide world worries (or thinks) non-stop. You'll face all kinds of prideful people. They'll make you think they've got this thing all figured out. But that's not so. We all worry. More than we realize. The best news is, though, that once you know that, and pull back the curtain and let the light unclothe the shadows, you'll begin to steady and resolve your jaded view. You're bringing forth God's goodness to the surface of your life where worry melts in the shower of his illuminated presence and warmth. You're beginning to *unlearn your worry.*

Peer through the darkness.

Return your eyes to the light.

Return your eyes to *him.*

REFLECTION QUESTIONS

1. Are you aware how much your thoughts are riddled with worry? What do they look like?

2. What worries have surfaced that consume you most? Why, why, and why? What fears have now surfaced?

3. How does it feel to bring your fears to the light? What keeps you from recognizing your worries, thus staying stuck in blind spots and leaving fear buried in the dark?

4. What truths of God do you know? How can you allow God's light to begin to dissolve your rooted fears?

THREE

UPROOT IT

Uncovering the True Enemy

"Bamboozled!" Mike interjected.

As the recipient of my overflowing convictions, my husband blurted this out while guzzling from my fire hose of uncontainable passion for the subject of this chapter. *Bamboozled . . .* Yes! Love it. Sounds cool, looks cool. The only thing not so cool is when it happens to you. Defined as "to deceive or get the better of (someone) by trickery, flattery, or the like,"[1] *bamboozled* more or less translates to "you're being lied to." No one wants to be played for a fool. Um . . . that's a big fat no thanks from me! In fact, of all the no-no's we have zero tolerance for in our household, "no lying" ranks near the top of our family commandments.

How about you? Have you ever been lied to, tricked, or bamboozled? Maybe you find this an easy yes or "are you kidding me?" But, if you have to rack your foggy brain over this one, let me help

---

[1]Dictionary.com, s.v. "bamboozle," accessed November 23, 2022, https://www.dictionary.com/browse/bamboozle.

you out. If you've worried (everyone, remember?), then you have been lied to.

Your worries and fears are, in fact, all lies.

How do I know? Because I happen to know the deceiver pumping out those lousy lies. Unfortunately. Who am I talking about? That would be the obnoxious snake we met in an opening scene of the Bible. Satan. Satan has been bamboozling you your entire existence, and we soften it by calling it worry. You've likely clued in to the character of Satan as the father of all lies (John 8:44). As in the author of lies and ultimate liar. Well, have you also heard that fear is a liar? Zach Williams wrote a whole song about this nasty truth. And to sum it up, if Satan is the lead liar, and it's true that fear is a liar, then fear would have to stem from Satan, right? Exactly. Since God is love, and perfect love casts out all fear, then God isn't the source of fear at all. It's straight from his opponent. Which means we can agree with Mr. Williams that fear (which we established is at the root of worry) is indeed a liar. Liar, aka Satan.

What I'm trying to highlight is this: When it comes to all your worrisome thoughts and fears, Satan is the true enemy on the attack. The actual one we need to be singling out and putting up our fight against.

> Fear is indeed a liar.
> Satan is the true enemy on the attack.

An ironic example struck me this morning.

I may be loaded with serious conviction about my disgust for the enemy and being lied to, and you'd think this would help me avoid being victimized by the stalking swindler. But he snuck up and fooled me the very day I was preparing to share these points with you.

Feeling pretty confident that "bamboozled" was my choice word to open this can of worms, I still found myself uncertain and unsure how to proceed. How should I string together a message justifying the ridiculous degree to which Satan is working us? I was stumped. And in my confusion and my neglect to consult God on the matter, my thoughts began to run wild. Smothering me with worry.

I don't know what you do when your brain gets crowded with contemplation, but I get the urge to run. Literally. Escape from my confined space so my messy mind can breathe deeper and thoughts can flow freer. I'm an overthinker, so this happens about daily for me. Brisk walks or quick jogs are my therapy. So, on this particular morning, I anxiously laced up my running shoes and bolted out the door with my muck of emotions under the early summer sun. Me, talking to me, about the father of lies . . .

What would I say? How would I say it? Would my words make sense? Would it have an impact? What if I fail? Tangled, misleading, misguided thoughts bombarded my mind as I pounded the pavement with continuous strides of worry.

Do you see what was happening? It almost stopped me in my breathless tracks. He had me. I was being bamboozled. Deceived by the liar. Deceived by the lying fear of failure.

Why the Lies?

Why would he do such a thing? Why all the deception and the lies? The answer to the *why* is what really ticks me off. It's this. He wants me to fail. And yep, he wants you to fail too. Whatever you're afraid of is provoking the enemy to pump out the heartiest happy dance. Think about it. If he can keep me worried, afraid, convinced I'll fail, and far from God, I might become paralyzed with fear and too debilitated to bust his cover.

You think Satan wants you to know what I'm telling you? That he's the enemy. You might then drop your worry like a bad habit and go out in the world and do some good. Ohhh, and that would not be good for Satan, my friend. He'd lose, and God would gain some serious ground. In fact, it's been about six weeks from the time I started this chapter until I finally found the words to make it more complete. He does not want me to talk about him. No ma'am, no sir. Nor does he want you to know that he is the actual enemy. But he doesn't give up. He pressed on in his quest to shake me up and break me down with all the fearful thoughts of failure. *Keri, you're not enough. Keri, you can't do this.* And I stalled.

When do you hear thoughts like this? Do you listen to the lies? (All worriers, hands up.) Pretty much, we're all being bamboozled one worry and fear at a time. I don't know about you, but that notion stirs up some serious fight in me. And maybe simply knowing you're being deceived as well will turn on lightbulbs and trigger a little more fight in your war with the deceiver. I hope it does. But I think we ought to crack this concept wide open so we can beef up our challenge against our feisty opponent.

> We're all being bamboozled one
> worry and fear at a time.

What Do You Really Believe?

Now no one would actually admit to believing a liar or trusting a bamboozler. No way. Most of us would claim we believe God, that HE is the only one to be trusted. But our shaky state of life contradicts what we say we believe, as we fall for and give in to worry. In reality, we are portraying belief and trust in the liar. Hurts, doesn't it?

So, what are the lies we're falling for? In the last chapter, the fears you whittled down to, at the bottom of your brain dump of worries, were the lies that you've been believing. It's quite possible this compiled a vast variety of root fears. And did the volume of struggles that surfaced bombard you? The thing is, it can be a smidge overwhelming trying to fight too many giants. For most of us, tackling too much simultaneously can confuse us and curb our capacity to overcome. We cave in defeat, becoming disabled. Blindsided by intense pressure. At least this is true of me. But, being prepared with quick comebacks when Satan sneaks up really does toughen my fight. I'd love the same for you. So, I decided to simplify some retaliation for us.

Before I go there, I want to share a sneak peek at what I found in my research. Secular psychology recognizes numerous negative self-beliefs. Beliefs, that as Christians, we can recognize as "lies," based on their direct opposite nature to God's truths. Lies that you'll find parallel with our worries and fears.

Here are some of those unfavorable beliefs:[2]

Inadequate	Unwanted	Ineffective
Unattractive	Incompetent	Different
Powerless	Uncared for	Defective
Undesirable	Weak	Don't Measure Up
Trapped	Bad	Not Good Enough
Rejected	Vulnerable	Loser
Inferior	Worthless	Out of Control
Alone	Failure	Damaged

[2] Judith S. Beck, *Cognitive Therapy: Basics and Beyond* (New York: Guilford, 1995).

To view this collection of pessimism from a higher level, Dr. Judith Beck, in *Cognitive Therapy for Challenging Problems*, simply suggests three negative core beliefs ("lies" from our Christian perspective) that all the other beliefs funnel into.[3] Belief in

> Helplessness
> Unlovability
> Worthlessness

And another broad opinion from licensed psychologist Dr. Maggie Perry references a slightly different set of three:[4]

> Helplessness
> Hopelessness
> Worthlessness

Now, though the four focus beliefs noted—helplessness, hopelessness, worthlessness, and unlovability—seem to represent these negative beliefs well and are commonly considered to sum up the larger, longer list of lies we believe, I propose we narrow it down even further. To two. Here's why. From a Christian viewpoint, it occurred to me that *hopelessness* points to *helplessness*, and similarly *unlovability* finds its root in the lie and fear of *worthlessness*. Like this:

> If I believe the lie of hopelessness, I am believing the lie of *helplessness*.

> If I believe the lie of unlovability, I am believing the lie of *worthlessness*.

---

[3] Judith S. Beck, *Cognitive Therapy for Challenging Problems: What to Do When the Basics Don't Work* (New York: Guilford, 2005).

[4] Maggie Perry, "Redirect Rumination," *Huddle.care Weekly,* October 20, 2019, https://huddlecareweekly.substack.com/p/redirect-rumination#details.

And even though the reports don't specifically single out fear and worry, the core beliefs, or lies we're speaking of here, are also what we worry about. Or what we fear. In our foundation.

I want you to look back at the expanded list of negative beliefs. *Inadequate, rejected, alone, uncared for, powerless, not good enough.* Aren't these the same as many of the worries and fears you've dug up?

Allow me to help you bunch up all your big bad worries and the lies you're believing (like the ones above) and pile them into just two "foundational fears" to prepare your optimal retaliation against the enemy. Go ahead. Jot down, flip back to, and recall some of your worries. Let's see if you can't trace them back to one of two fears:

Fear of Helplessness
Fear of Worthlessness

If I could sit with you and all your mental and scribbled notes, I bet we'd find "Fear of Helplessness" or "Fear of Worthlessness" at the root. Hard to believe? Let's test it out.

Example: You have super-exciting-to-you news to share with your best friend. But you start to feel unsure she'll even care. Hello, worry! Maybe she'll suppose you're annoying, boasting, or monopolizing the conversation. Okay, well, what are you so worried about here? What are you fearful of? Feeling let down by her lack of excitement, maybe?

You then walk through the practice we learned in Chapter Two to figure out the fear at the root or these festering worries. And you detect *a fear of what people think about you.* But, after diving even deeper, you decide it's rooted in some sort of *fear of rejection.* I can see that. I can relate for sure.

But is that really as deep as the fear goes?

Another example. You are a master worrier about your teenage child or husband's safety on the road. Worried about the weather, who's driving the car, how fast they'll fly down the highway, and whether they have a horrible habit of texting while driving. And when you got to the bottom of the pit of asking yourself *why* (*Why am I worried about that?*) again and again, you see these worries must point to a fear of losing a loved one. Or even deeper, a *fear of being alone. Loneliness.* I can also relate to that.

But again, is that as deep as the fear goes?

It's not.

Both are definitely examples of relevant fears. But if you dig even deeper, asking *why* one more time *(Why do I fear rejection when sharing the news with my friend?)*, you might discover you fear *rejection* because you ultimately fear being *unworthy.* Feeling the lack of being valued by others. Fear of worthlessness.

Or, in the case with your spouse and kids' safety, the reality beyond the fear of loneliness *(Why do I fear being alone if something happens to a loved one?)* is that we ultimately fear being *helpless.* Feeling our lack of ability to control outcomes. Fear of helplessness.

With each fear you've named, ask yourself: Could it be because I fear being *helpless*? Or . . . do I fear this because I fear being *worthless*?

Placing a confident finger on one of these two primary fears, or maybe both, as the source of each worry will help you strategically spot powerful comebacks to pinpoint and fight your fiery thoughts. The enemy. I hope you'll take a sec to reflect on the list a few pages back, the two foundational fears, and decide which you relate to most.

Do your thoughts show you struggle with . . .
Fear of rejection?

Fear of abandonment?
Fear of undesirability?
Fear of unlovability?
Fear of being unwanted, uncared for, or undeserving?
At the root you'll likely find a fear of worthlessness.

Do your worries reveal you wrestle with . . .
Fear of physical pain?
Fear of discomfort?
Fear of loneliness?
Fear of hopelessness?
Fear of failure, being powerless or incompetent?
At the foundation you'll probably find a fear
of helplessness.

> **Whatever you fear, don't forget,
> they're all deceptions**

Foundational Fibs

Friend, whatever you fear, don't forget, they're all deceptions.
When we live with a tent pitched over any worry, camped out on
the fear of helplessness or worthlessness, we are believing one of
two lies (sometimes both). To help etch them into your memory
(I'd like to think my crafty alliteration can assist), I'll refer to your
foundational fears (lies) by calling them "Foundational Fibs." I'm
sort of being soft, subtle, and kind by labeling them fibs, because
they are more like conniving, crooked, fictitious phrases. But the
fibs you are believing are these:
   I am helpless.
   I am worthless.

Low blow. You'd never tell someone you're these things. Imagine this. A bunch of us introducing ourselves at church on Sunday to a newcomer. "Hey there, I'm 'helpless.' Sometimes I call myself 'worthless.'" That definitely wouldn't make you any quick friends. But deep in your core, in the fluster of your foundation, this is what you're believing. All the worry you rehashed says so. What a rat that Satan is in manipulating us into believing such lies. And what's worse is that we are giving in to his trickery. I'd say we've had enough. You?

"The voice of the Snake is gentle; his opening remarks straightforward and seemingly harmless. With a whisper, he weaves doubt and fear into a shawl and then gracefully drapes it over Eve's shoulders." Malinda Fuller opened my eyes wide with a glimpse of the liar's character in her book, *Obedience over Hustle*.[5] Oh, he is ever so brilliant in his vindictive ways.

The last thing any of us wants is to be naïve and gullible to a trickster. But, if he's gotten us to fall for his deception since he tempted Eve in the garden of Eden, and has continued to succeed with his masked charm without our notice ever since, he's not giving up anytime soon. How can we see through his façade? How can we stand up against the enemy that has proven relentless?

Recognizing the Enemy

It's the absolute truth; he is relentless. Ruthlessly relentless. He is wildly determined to win the war over the truth and over our thoughts. He's a master bamboozler.

We've got to be on the lookout constantly. We need to learn to decipher his angles. And if being better aware of his nature helps us fight, what do you say we zoom in on some of his key

---

[5]Malinda Fuller, *Obedience over Hustle: The Surrender of the Striving Heart* (Uhrichsville, OH: Shiloh Run, 2019), 85.

characteristics to watch out for so we can prepare to resist and fire back? Check this out:

1. **The enemy is deceitful.** "This great dragon—the ancient serpent called the devil, or Satan, the one deceiving the whole world—was thrown down to the earth with all his angels" (Rev. 12:9 NLT). Make no mistake, Satan is deceiving. The "whole world." Not one of us will be immune to his deception on this side of heaven. If you smell or taste worry, know you are being deceived and can chalk it up as false. Out with it!

2. **The enemy is skilled.** "Now the serpent was more crafty than any other beast of the field that the LORD God had made" (Gen. 3:1 ESV). "Your enemy the devil prowls around like a lion looking for someone to devour" (1 Pet. 5:8). Can't you picture it? Smart, sneaky, trolling around for his prey. And seeking out a vulnerable victim makes the enemy's attack a much greater success. That's us. I see this in my own life a whole lot more than I want to admit. He totally ambushes me when I'm down. Think about it. You're super busy, overwhelmed. That's when my clarity's faint, and his twisted lies begin to look legit. How about sleep deprived, discouraged, sick, or sad? In this tender space we're easily confused into thinking our fears are valid. Perfect time to strike. Yes, clever. But don't fall for it!

3. **The enemy is fierce and hateful.** "The thief comes only to steal and kill and destroy" (John 10:10). "The devil has come down to you in great wrath, because he knows that his time is short!" (Rev. 12:12 ESV). Yep, expect a fierce fight. He knows you're hungry for what's good, what's right, and what's pure. And that makes Satan crazy mad.

There's not an ounce of love in him. He's straight-up vicious. So, no, your worry is never in love, and your fear is not for your protection. It's for the villain's minimizing of good and of God. He can come on so strong, upper-cutting you with fear and swift attacks that aim to squash truth and derail any progress you're making in God's kingdom. Let that light a fire in you. Not today, Satan!

4. **The enemy is subtle.** Satan is a sly, inconspicuous tempter—"And no wonder, for even Satan disguises himself as an angel of light" (2 Cor. 11:14 ESV). An angel, really? Of light? If he can be so incognito that we think he's an angel of light, we're in big trouble. In terms of worry, it may creep past undistinguishable. He nudges and drips tiny temptations of stress so smoothly, making you even entertain the error it's in your best interest to worry. Satan dribbles disguised, itty-bitty, seemingly safe and harmless worries that snowball into big fears until you succumb, avoiding life. Void of joy and the great purpose God has for you. Keep a close eye on your small, subtle worries. Don't let a trace go unnoticed!

5. **The enemy is powerful.** "We know that we are from God, and the whole world lies in the power of the evil one" (1 John 5:19 ESV). Yikes. That right there would be a scary scripture. If. If you only fixed your focus on what comes after the comma. The key here is "world." When we are of the world, yes, we slump under Satan's power. But remember, you are from God. If you're conformed to what the world wants and says, you're going to fall victim to this intrusive power. Don't do it! Buckle up your faith belt! You can resist the liar, fight the fear, and conquer the enemy. Let's look at how.

God Has the Ultimate Power

The enemy may be deceitful, skilled, hateful, subtle, and unfortunately powerful. BUT GOD. God is so much more. God is so much greater than our enemy. God is truth. God is wisdom and the way. He is love and life. He provides a way out. And he is infinitely *all*-powerful. And *you*, my dear, precious, prized child of God, have access to him.

> "Little children (believers, dear ones), you are of God and you belong to Him and have [already] overcome them [the agents of the antichrist]; because He who is in you is greater than he (Satan) who is in the world [of sinful mankind]." (1 John 4:4 AMP)

This is amazing news!

1. **God is truth.** "The sum of your word is truth, and every one of your righteous rules endures forever" (Ps. 119:160 ESV). "So Jesus said to the Jews who had believed him, 'If you abide in my word, you are truly my disciples, and you will know the truth, and the truth will set you free'" (John 8:31–32 ESV). God is nothing but honest. The absolute opposite of what you get from the enemy. So, you best believe it. God can be trusted. One hundred percent. And you can trust the Bible. One hundred percent. I love the part that declares "the truth will set you free." Isn't that what you want? Freedom? I do! Freedom from the liar, freedom from the worry, freedom from the fear? Well, there is freedom in the truth of God. Run hard after it and claim your freedom, friend!

2. **God is the way.** The wise way. "Oh, the depth of the riches and wisdom and knowledge of God! How unsearchable are His judgments and decisions and

how unfathomable and untraceable are His ways!"
(Rom. 11:33 AMP). Satan may have expert skills in stirring
up worry and breaking you down until fear convinces
you there's no way out. But God is the way. He is wiser,
and he can restore even the things Satan drags you down
with. "And the God of all grace, who called you to his
eternal glory in Christ, after you have suffered a little
while, will himself restore you and make you strong,
firm and steadfast" (1 Pet. 5:10). Because of God, there
is always hope. It may be unfathomable to you if you've
been living with worry your whole life. But, no matter
how deep the enemy knocks you down in the dumps or
how stuck you feel, God can restore you and raise you
back up.

3. **God is love.** And full life. Where the first half of this
scripture reveals Satan as a thief coming to steal and
destroy, the good stuff follows—"I have come that they
may have life, and have it to the full" (John 10:10). "God
is love" (1 John 4:8). This is my most favorite characteris-
tic of God. Better than that, God is perfect love. He gives
this flawless love to give us full life. And a life full of
worry and fear is not the kind of full life he had in mind.
It's missing his perfect love. If we could grasp how madly
God loves us, what in the world would we have to fear?
The answer is *nothing*. Because no matter what happens,
you can trust you'll be taken care of. With perfect love.
How much does a mother love her new sweet-smelling
baby? She would give her life for this gift, who has nothing to worry about under her abounding love and care.
And here's something else for you. That doesn't even
begin to compare to how loved you are by your heavenly
Father. He's got you covered. Smothered. Let this soak

into you, soothe you, bless you. And then watch worry melt down as Satan slinks away.

4. **God provides a way out.** He is the answer. "No temptation has overtaken you except what is common to mankind. And God is faithful; he will not let you be tempted beyond what you can bear. But when you are tempted, he will also provide a way out so you can endure it" (1 Cor. 10:13). When worry waltzes in and whisks you away into temptation and trouble, have no fear, he is near. Forever faithful. God will always offer a solution to your worries. Praise him for that!

5. **God is ALL-powerful.** This is the greatest news of all time. God, who is in you, is greater than Satan and all his horrid traits (1 John 4:4). Truth. And through God we have the power to fight and fend off all the fear and worry Satan slings at us. "Submit yourselves, then, to God. Resist the devil, and he will flee from you" (James 4:7). He will flee. Can I get a Hallelujah!? Bye-bye, Satan.

> God will always offer a solution to your worries.

God Is the Trusted Truth

You and I can't trust a trace or whisper of our worry and fear. Because they're all lies. The truth is, God is the only one we can trust. The only one. I've given you lots of illustrations and ways he is wiser, stronger, and the one to be trusted. But I promised a practice to help you better retain them.

If we can simply key in on two Trusted Truths to combat the two Foundational Fibs and become intimately familiar with them, we just might stand bolder and firmer against the deceit. I chose only two truths to equally match the foundational fears and fibs for good reason. Though I've recited hundreds of solid biblical truths and plugged them in to the fibers of my thoughts, I still find it easier to get lost and fumble through than do a quick pick from one of the many weapons available. Truly, before I land on the most effective ammunition, it's not uncommon to get sidelined and distracted pondering all the potential choices to charge back with. Periodically to the point of getting cast completely off course by the enemy's temptation and charm. But, when we simply have two loaded missiles to launch, we can ready-aim-fire so fast the enemy doesn't stand a chance.

Ready for them? Let's load up.

Trusted Truth #1—I have help.
Trusted Truth #2—I am worthy.

These two phrases are your new best friends. Fear and worry are your worst enemies, and "I have help" and "I am worthy" are there to protect you. Whatever the teeny-tiny worry is that sneaks up behind you in the carpool line, or the big obnoxious fear that jumps into your traffic path on the way to work, or whatever worrisome thoughts throw punches at you day after day after day. Whether your fear is rooted in helplessness (I am helpless) or in worthlessness (I am worthless), tearing down those lies with these two trusted truths has the power to smother the anxious, debilitating enemy.

You have the authority to voice and live the win over worry because of what Jesus has done in overcoming the enemy, by defeating death on the cross. It's because of his sacrifice, his power, that we can conquer the liar. So, repeating and believing these two phrases in the face of any worry or any fear can crush Satan. Let's practice.

> You have the authority to voice and live the win over worry because of what Jesus has done in overcoming the enemy, by defeating death on the cross.

I have help. You are not helpless. I repeat. You are never help-less. Because you have God. Always. Simple as that. He's there to help you and will never leave you. You may not always acknowl-edge it, but he's there nonstop with his help. So, no matter where the worry and fear may take you—facing the fear of death of a loved one, your own declining health or financial ruin, fear of flying, or just plain fear of fear—you can shout in your heart or out loud with your lungs, "With God, I am never helpless. I always have help!"

> I lift up my eyes to the mountains—where does my help come from? My help comes from the LORD, the Maker of heaven and earth. He will not let your foot slip—he who watches over you will not slumber; indeed, he who watches over Israel will neither slumber nor sleep. The LORD watches over you—the LORD is your shade at your right hand; the sun will not harm you by day, nor the moon by night. The LORD will keep you from all harm—he will watch over your life; the LORD will watch over your coming and going both now and forevermore. (Ps. 121)

Now and forevermore. I'll hold on to that one.

> "With God, I am never helpless. I always have help!"

I am worthy. You are so, so incredibly loved by your Father. And you are wonderfully worthy because his love covers you perfectly. He made you. So, if worry takes you down the dark road to fear of rejection, failure, loneliness, being unloved, or ultimately to worthlessness, you can toss the enemy a big fat "Peace out!" And declare, "I am loved larger than I can possibly imagine with a love that fills fuller than I could possibly imagine. And that makes me more worthy than absolutely anything the enemy tries to take away." But you've got to own it and claim it in the face of the deceptive worry Satan hurls at you. You can fire back with this, "Because of God's perfect love for me, I am always worthy." And guess what?! No one can separate you from that. No one.

> And I am convinced that nothing can ever separate us from God's love. Neither death nor life, neither angels nor demons, neither our fears for today nor our worries about tomorrow—not even the powers of hell can separate us from God's love. (Rom. 8:38 NLT)

> And that is what some of you were. But you were washed, you were sanctified, you were justified in the name of the Lord Jesus Christ and by the Spirit of our God. (1 Cor. 6:11)

> Because of God's perfect love for me,
> I am always worthy.

The Bible is stacked full of so much more Scripture backing up these truths. This is just a taste to hold you over. I hope you search and find far more.

What's Next?

Embarrassed to confess this, but I honestly once thought if I acknowledged Satan, he'd be more likely to stick around. Or worse, come closer. Kind of like an annoying little brother that hears mention of his name and nags, "Did I hear you talking about me?" and then amps up his pestering. (I'm not talking about you, bro. Love ya!)

Can you relate? This isn't the way it happens, though. Remember, if you resist the archenemy, he'll actually flee from you. True statement.

I understand it's hard to admit and face the fact we're constantly up against an enemy. It's a heavy weight to carry. But if we can't come to grips with this reality, we'll find it terribly tough to fight back at him. Don't make the mistake of minimizing Satan like I have. We should take super seriously the need to stay on guard and ward him off. Because as much as I desperately wish I could prove otherwise, he is real.

But here's something else I want to make crystal clear. We shouldn't give him too much credit either. Because GOD gets the ultimate credit. May you never forget that God is more powerful. May you never forget you have the power (with God in you) to kick Satan to the curb at any moment worry and fear try to trip you. You do.

So, while Satan's been on your coattails, bamboozling you, teaching you about worry, forcing fear on you, you have a much stronger power within. God's power. To remind you how worthy you are, and to assure you that you are never helpless. Because God is the ultimate victor. Tapped in to his love and power, with his love and power, you can always beat down the enemy. Always.

GOD wins.

Period.

· ·

God is the ultimate victor.

· ·

REFLECTION QUESTIONS

1. How is Satan bamboozling you with worry? Are you falling for his lies?

2. Do your worries and fears indicate you are believing the Foundational Fibs that you are helpless, worthless, or both? How?

3. How do you feel about God's Trusted Truths? Do you believe you are always worthy and never helpless?

4. Do you give Satan credit for the worry in your life? Can you accept and acknowledge that God's power is greater?

FOUR

UNLOAD IT
Lifting It Up in Prayer

I am skeptical.

By way of illustration, you'll have a tough time convincing me you've caught glimpses of ghosts, I rarely trust gas station strangers with dark hoodies draped over their heads, and when it comes to any national news channel, I just know there's a hidden agenda that strictly includes manipulating the general public for the growth of some bigwig's pocketbook.

Skeptical.

Do we happen to share this common trait? At all? I have a hunch we might if you can admit "worrier" ever describes your disposition. And it makes perfect sense, because where worry lurks, skepticism trails close behind.

Well, I hope you aren't skeptical of this chapter. I probably would be. It's highly possible when browsing a table of contents in a book about worry that the "prayer" chapter would signal a "no, duh" and a "yeah, right." Like, *I've tried that. I've prayed myself silly, and the wretched worry won't budge. Okay, let's see whatcha got, Eichberger!* (That's Ike-Burger, by the way)

Don't be skeptical. Grande order for skeptics, I know. But I really think you'll find this to be different. If you're up for it, I'd like to take you somewhere you've maybe never been with this. I'm going to challenge you. I'm going to challenge me.

We're not doing enough.

We're not.

Oh, great. Right? Someone to judge and assume they know. Now you're more skeptical.

I get it. And I know I don't have a clue about what goes on in your prayer life, but there's something in the Bible that I've found rather peculiar. A specific scripture that I now think deserves more of a triple than even merely a double take.

It's in Thessalonians. And it reads "Pray continually" (1 Thess. 5:17). Or as the ESV puts it, "Pray without ceasing." If this is a guide for how we should pray (which I believe it is), how would you say you measure up? I'll tell you how I fare. *Meh.* Not so close to a perfect score, that's for sure. I'd like to present myself a good ole pat on the back for genuine effort, but I think what this truly means here is, literally, *nonstop.* The only thing I've admitted to doing nonstop is *thinking.*

I talk to God, chat through dilemmas with Jesus, and hold inner dialogue with the Holy Spirit about a hundred checkpoints a day (not bad, right?). But *continually*? Sorry. Can't say I do. There are loads of stops and starts. And so, as for the heaps of in-betweens, Lord, help us all, amen? Highway to the danger zone of thought-scurry and worry.

If you can confess to prayer disruptions too (come on, admit it), you're with the 110 percent rest of us. The privileged whole of humanity that have the blessed opportunity to pray that much *more* and dip into even greater aid, relief, and (I bet) extremely welcome burden lifting of the worries messing with you today.

Based on where we've traveled so far, if you dove deep enough below the surface of your everyday worries and excavated the fears at your foundation, you'd find a large part of unlearning worry is in lifting it up where it belongs. With God. In prayer. Letting it go . . . to God.

Think Elsa in the famous scene from *Frozen*, belting out that notorious tune. "Let it go, let it go . . ." as she thrashes out her pent-up power through her fingertips, freeing her, empowering her shackled soul. Imagine you, unloading, whipping out your worries far, far away and into God's care. Over and over. All of it. Yes! It's time to let it all go.

Prayer is the avenue of releasing our cares to the only One worthy of working out our worry. The One who can turn it into good. And turn it around toward freedom.

If you're open and ready, I have three key prayer concepts I want to place in your heart as we settle in on the power of prayer. Three ideas that I think may encourage your frequency and the fruitfulness of your open conversations with the Lord. They are (1) Never stop praying, (2) God listens, and (3) God answers.

> Prayer is the avenue of releasing our cares to the only One worthy of working out our worry.

Never Stop Praying

We touched on the "big man's" instruction to pray continually, which is the first key worth mentioning. But, I want to expand on *how* before I lead you to *why* this one is so important (answered in numbers two and three).

I had a brilliant idea. (I thought.)

What more creative way to prove the roadblocks and barriers to successfully praying all day than to draw an image for you of the mania I'm smushed in right now. And, oh yeah, let me tell ya, it was feeling oh so satisfying when I started slinging the kernels of my crazy into an overflowing repository of madness to spring forth. But then, I decided I'd spare you.

Who am I kidding? You don't need me to paint a picture of what a frenzy looks like. In fact, no one wants to hear my pity party of what's wild and wacky. You've got your very own front-row seat, high-definition-3D-view of a life bursting with busy. You're writing your own chapter on that. And this yo-yo full calendar is exactly what makes our prayer life so hit-or-miss and choppy half the time. Or all the time over here. You too?

First Fruits First

So, we've got to start the day on the offense. Seriously, as soon as your slumbering dreams wake to "what day is it?" or whatever auto-thought sweetly greets you in the morning, *pray*. Kind of corny maybe, but I've gotten in the habit of mental song before I open my eyes to the dim light. "This is the day that the Lord has made, I will rejoice and be glad in it . . ." Totally 1980s VBS style, but it puts Jesus on my mind first. And that is the point. That is a start.

Then a stop. Ugh. See how quickly we screw this up? Just don't take it a step further off track and pick up a tech device before your next encounter with God. (Guilty.) You can keep singing your way to the potty (we still say that at my house with toddlers, sorry), but your next goal is to surrender your first fifteen minutes (your first fruits) to God in prayer, void of distraction and Satan's attempts to steer you off. Way off.

My friend Sue reminds me how foolish I am when I forget this. She's the kind of crazy-for-Jesus gal every soul should cling to, exploding with affirmation and encouragement. But she shoots straight when it comes to this topic. "Don't be a fool, Keri," she reminds me when referencing her passion on giving the Lord your first fifteen minutes of the day. I'm pretty sure she borrowed this catchphrase from our pastor, but she snatched it up and gets so fired up spilling it like the latest and greatest news. And I think she's on to something. Don't be a fool! Don't be bamboozled. Start your day with God.

Here's an idea. This thought totally just bubbled up, so I haven't tried it, but it might be genius—who knows! Send me a DM on Insta and let me know if it worked for you. So, this: Slap a sticky note on your phone before you go to bed that reads "Don't be a fool!" Wonder if that will keep your hands off. Report back, will you?

> **Don't be a fool! Don't be bamboozled.
> Start your day with God.**

Don't Forget

In a fit of fervor, Sue most recently followed her "don't be a fool" statement with something like "And if you get this right, you'll fly high with God all day." I love her excitement, but my skepticism was thinking, *Yeah, until one of the multitude of things I was kind enough not to dump on you jumps out in front of me and smacks me square between the eyes. So much for flying high.* Crash and burn. You know what I'm talking about? Surprises. You name it. Life's full of them.

That's why it's imperative that my first fifteen minutes includes this particular prayer. *Lord, help me to not forget you.* I'm saying when the unforeseen objects fly in front of my face and the wind is sucked from my sails, and I'm not soaring so much anymore, *I need you, God.* Pray. *Don't let me forget you, God.* Pray hard.

Pray hard? If that's possible, I do it. I pray it, say it, repeat it, pause on it, feel it deep in my soul. I *pleeeeead* with him, "Lord, please, oh please, oh please, oh *pleeeeease* don't let me forget you. When something comes up, I want to make you the first thing I see, the One I turn my pleas and thoughts to. No one else. Nothing else. You. Don't let me forget your trusted truths. Place them hard on my heart." Praying hard. And harder. Deeply and convicted. This sort of strong start is absolutely pivotal in opening spiritual chat lines for the rest of the day.

Change Up

If you truly want to go deeper, richer, and clear the path to more constant awareness of his presence, you'll probably need to change some things in the day ahead. Listen, I know. It's not easy to keep communication going all day with God. You've got hardwired habits and routines, and they've been met with repeated thoughts that may not include space for free-flow spiritual thinking. But if we're going to continue to win over worry, we've got to be open to learning some new stuff to replace the old. All part of the unlearning process.

So what can you adjust? The goal is to pray more to worry less, so if you're serious about this, I've got some change-ups that were seriously effective for me, which might be worth your try.

Drop the phone. I am totally hot and cold on this one, I can't lie. I've had some seriously successful seasons of not giving my cell so much as a glance the first waking hour of my day. But lately, it's like I have this anxious twitch. Satan pestering me. Jealous of the lack of attention he's been noticing.

I started placing my phone on my dresser across the room when I went to bed. And I'll tell you, that was a super solution to keep my arm from reaching over and slapping the nightstand before my eyes even opened. But it was only a matter of time before the enemy upped his game and allowed my brain to teach my legs to autopilot to my device as my arm had learned. I suppose I ought to move technology to the closet or outside my bedroom door. Hey, that "Don't be a fool" sticky note would be helpful here! Either way, if you want to make a serious effort to give God your undivided attention, remove, move, or alter the distraction.

Turn down the noise. Music can be lovely. A beautiful form of worship. And there is a time and place for the TV too. But for me, when pressing toward spending more time in prayer, with the purpose of unloading my particular cares to the Lord, keeping the sound off on morning jogs or afternoon carpool can provide quiet space to chat with God about my specific struggles. The silence allows me to pinpoint the exact thoughts and troubles taking hold of me. Create more calm and quiet. Talk to God there. It's a habit worth getting into.

Turn up the music. Sometimes our auto-thoughts are *no bueno*. So, as much as we want to naturally focus on the junk we need to hand over in prayer, at times we need to force-feed our thinkers the goodness of God. That is, to even begin to focus on what needs fixing. For this, I'm going to suggest the slight opposite. Turn *on* some music. Or turn over the music if you're drowning (or even escalating) your cares in something like country music (no disrespect). But, flip the switch to contemporary Christian or classic hymns. Whatever floats your fancy that triggers thought sorting with God. Allowing you to pass soothing truths over your aching soul. Crank it up in the car. Pop in some earbuds while sweeping the kitchen floor, replying to emails, watering the flowers, walking to the mailbox, or prepping dinner. Plant these musical reminders to sift through the fears and frustrations of the hour. Nourish your thought space with God's words and God's voice, opening more continual communication, slowly crushing the enemy's constant chirp of worry.

> Nourish your thought space with God's words and God's voice, opening more continual communication, slowly crushing the enemy's constant chirp of worry.

Pray yourself to sleep. You may think this sounds sacrilegious or something. But hear me out on this one. How many times have you laid your head on your pillow at night with the struggle bus of thinking whipping wildly through your mind? It might be the next day's craze, the conflict with one of your kids at the dinner table, the stirring tension with your spouse in the bathroom during the nightly teeth brushing, the heavy heart for the piled-up prayer requests. Or maybe you're swelling with guilt that you totally flopped at the whole talk-to-God-all-day fantasy.

You're filled with consuming weariness of the brain. You need rest and you need him. So, borrow this, my most favorite prayer tip of the day. Lay down your sweet head, close your tired eyes, and begin pouring it all out. I bet you'll fall asleep faster. And if you don't, just take it as God wanting to hear more of what you've got and wanting you to release it into his care. I'm telling you, you'll wake tomorrow as if you had an overnight counseling session. The Lord is so good like that.

Change Is Worth It

This "without ceasing" thing is no joke, but if you can give God your start, plan plenty of checkpoints throughout the day, and finish with him, you'll become more used to hashing out your every emotion with your should-be go-to. And this is regardless of how worried or fearful you might feel. True, if you're having a horrendously hard time letting go of a stubborn struggle, you might want to take the "continually" command a bit more literally, knowing you'll get as much out of it as you put in. But even if you don't feel super weighed down, these practices are not only pleasing to God but will also firm up your fight the next time it wears thin. You'll be more rehearsed and ready for the win. So, jot down your "don't be a fool" note to self, crank up Lauren Daigle (my fave!), and practice with me.

God Listens

Do you ever think about the fact that when you pray, God is truly listening? In the Bible, Jeremiah 29:12 tells us when we call out to God in prayer, he listens. So, it's a fact. And the fact also is, we all want to be heard. We have so much inside stuffing us full of overwhelm and inescapable discouragement, defeat, and confusion, with not enough reliable sources to off-load it on. True? Well, thank God for *God*. It's a mystery why we don't rely on him more often, as we should.

> When you pray, God is truly listening.

People go to great extremes to be heard, paying big money to hammer out their every problem with someone. And since we're over here aiming to talk to God nonstop, we've got great news in our access to a constant listener. At our disposal at all times. Mind you, with no judgment, and he just so happens to love us more than anyone in the whole wide world. Dream come true. Why aren't we obsessing over running to him? What's wrong with us? Hey, I'm with you. I've gotten way better at this, but half the time, as soon as my mind starts racing with stress and struggle, I dial my mom, yell down to the basement to Mike, or vent in comments on a "who needs prayer post" on social media. Oops.

Friend in Jesus

I witnessed a tear-filled testimony from my friend Victoria yesterday, who gets it. Sitting around the table at our current Bible study on the Gospel of Mark, I asked the table what they've noticed from their new prayer structure—something we're focusing on this session. Her sweet response flooded my heart with all the "amens!" "I've noticed since I've started spending more time with God in the morning, talking to him, listening to him through nature, the birds, and sounds, I no longer feel like I'm just talking to God. I feel like I'm talking to my best friend." My smiles squeezed tears over my lower lids right with her. I get it. He's become my best friend too. A best friend I can always talk to. One who always listens.

> Since I've started spending more time with God in the morning, talking to him, listening to him through nature, the birds, and sounds, I no longer feel like I'm just talking to God. I feel like I'm talking to my best friend.

If you haven't sensed this kind of friend in Jesus, would you try to picture him right beside you? Picture him visibly next to you. You're starting your first fifteen minutes with him. You'll likely want that fifteen minutes to turn to thirty. Then before you know it, you're like me and ready to pour the biggest cup of coffee, call it quits on the rest of life, and sit with him all day.

If only it were that simple, huh? But really, see him with you. Take him with you. What does he look like? How does his still, patient, open-book presence make you feel? It's just you and him.

And he's listening to your every care and concern. You're releasing. And he comforts and calms to the core.

Get Alone

Speaking of deep conversations with your closest friends, you can probably attest to your richest encounters blooming from one-on-one time with them. Group gatherings are so important, as are community fellowship and worship. But deep heart connection happens when you give your 100 percent to the one you're communing with. You're alone.

I love to run with my husband. I also remember times past when I would solo soak in God's greatness around me and hear his sweet subtle signals just for me. Free from the wonder of expectation of someone beside me. But after a cold season hibernating away from the winter pavement, my fresh spring attempts to jog found me alongside my personal cheerleader and accountability partner. I truly enjoyed it. Until last Monday, when he was nursing a temporary injury and I was forced back out on the road alone. And just where I needed to be.

Me and God. Alone.

I didn't even have to be the one to strike up the conversation. I ventured out without the noise. As I stepped away from distractions one foot at a time, he began singing. My senses were aroused to his grandeur, majesty, and sweetness in intricate detail. Thankfulness slipped from the lips of my thoughts, followed by the melting of struggles from just seconds before into his worry-free creation.

This doesn't happen when I have a running partner. I'm blessed with good company, and I'll continue to invite Mike along, but I'd venture to say it's hard for God to hear us if we aren't talking to him. Maybe. It's hard to talk to one friend when you're trying to commit to the other stepping alongside you.

I love the imagery Mark conveys.

> Very early in the morning, while it was still dark, Jesus
> got up, left the house and went off to a solitary place,
> where he prayed. (Mark 1:35)

Jesus understood the need to be alone to pray. He understood
distractions. He apparently also understood the first-fruits notion.
He valued the richness gained from the quality time spent isolated
with his Father. It seems to have worked out pretty well for Jesus.
I'd like to follow him.

> **He valued the richness gained from the
> quality time spent isolated with his Father.**

What to Say

You're alone now and don't know what to say. He listens to all of it,
but I get the space cadet feeling of "where do I start?" and "what
do I unload first?" I really don't think you can mess up conversation with our nonjudgmental, unconditionally loving friend. But
it might be worth noting some guidance we got way back when
the Lord's Prayer was modeled in the Gospels. To keep it simple
and help your memory, how about my triple A's? *Awe, Ask, Admit.*

If you examine the Lord's Prayer, you'll see that Jesus encouraged a combination of these three identifiers. "Awe," reverence,
acknowledgment, appreciation, and thankfulness to God; "Ask,"
requests or petitions to God for basic needs or desires; and "Admit,"
confessions and concessions of our will to walk our own way and
voicing our need for deliverance.

There's something about starting our conversation out in *awe*,
admiration, and praise for who God is and what he has done that
takes the edge off the trial before it even finds its way to the *ask*
portion. Sure, it's the *ask* that most of us are truly after. We think

that's where God does the real work. And that would make sense too. But dolloping doses of God's greatness on top of the worries you're passing off to him have a divine way of diminishing those worries immediately.

Admit you've not done things perfectly his way, that he deserves so much more credit, and you want so badly to get it right. But it's fine to almost simultaneously *ask*, share, tell him what's really got you down, and express what you honestly want. He's listening. And just like bringing your fears to light began shedding their power, when you put God in his proper place amidst your requests, his presence diminishes the power of all your cares as he listens with love.

If you still feel unorganized, like a jumbled mess of I-don't-know-what-to-pray and I'm-no-good-at-this-stuff, pick up a pen.

> Dolloping doses of God's greatness on top of the worries you're passing off to him have a divine way of diminishing those worries immediately.

Write It Out

Just write. Jot down a prayer list. You can plot out the three A's or just bullet your worries. Even if you think you're not a good writer. I know lots like you. You've told me. But you can't mess this up. No one has to see. Scrunch it up and trash it afterward if you must, but trust me, it helps. You can search stats on the benefits of writing down, writing *out* (like it's literally coming out of you, unloading from you) what's on your mind to help ease the tension. Notice I'm not calling it journaling. That word makes some people cringe. Fine. You're not journaling, you're scribbling out fragments of thoughts. You can do this.

Meditate on It

If the heavy weight isn't lightening as you jot down the junk that's pressing on you that given day, sit with it. Sit on it. Mediate on it. Meaning what exactly? All this new age word really means to me in this context is to focus intently on each specific concern. Probably eyes closed. Minus distractions. Alone. As still as possible. Slower than you're used to. Staring at each word. Pausing. Waiting. For God to respond. Visualize handing it over. Acknowledging one word (pause), at a time (pause), how God is showing up in that very cluster of letters to shed light on your seeking soul.

You're reading your prayers. You're free-flow expanding your thoughts. You're praying over them. And you're praying over and over.

God Answers

Through each move with your new best friend, each prompt toward more conversation where the Lord listens, each practice of writing and reading over your words to God, something amazing happens. The focus shifts off self. The Holy Spirit comforts with a clearer abundant reality, and hope can grow here. Your perspective is redirected to God's promise of a good future as he opens his voice with answers.

And this, my friend, is what is so sweet about our time spent with the Lord. It's worth it. It's not wasted. Not only does God listen, but he also answers our prayers. And his answers are perfect. Right after Jeremiah 29:12 tells us that the Lord listens, verse 13 assures us we will find him when we seek him. Yes, it's in the finding him that you find his answers.

So, as we're going about our way praying all the livelong day, we are seeking God. And the Word of God says we'll find him there. We'll hear back from him. He will answer. But. I have a giant disclaimer to commercial break with. The answers don't always show up packaged at our front door the way we picture, with Amazon Prime delivery speed. You won't always get what you wish for. But you'll always end up with what God knows you need.

> **Not only does God listen, but he also answers our prayers. And his answers are perfect.**

What You Need

This may not encourage you. You want what you want. Or what you think you need. And when something else interjects its unwelcome self, you're left perplexed, puzzled, discouraged. I was there. Really, I've been there again and again. And more.

Last September I finally released the idea of this book to more Christian publishers than I knew existed and embarked on a supposed three-month wait for "the one." I was excited. I had marked my world with confident faith and "whatever you will, God." But worry fought hard to wriggle its way in. I held back the anxious urge to check my email every ten minutes. No exaggeration, maybe more.

A couple of "no's" trickled in. I suppressed tears with confidence that God had another perfect person in mind for me to team up with to make the most of the message on my heart. "It only takes one," I would remind myself. But the more I checked, the more worried I became. And discouraged. Three semitolerable *not now*s turned to ten painful *nos*. Then at the three-month mark, almost fifteen *who do you think you are*s (the story the rejections became in my head). That sneaky snake began to chew through me with worry this book might never happen. I must have heard God all wrong and am going to look like a big fat loser for putting myself out there proclaiming "I am writing a book."

And I prayed. More. I began to seek God harder, deeper. I lingered longer in my alone time. I wrote out my words of longing. I hung my head in surrender. I thanked him for the opportunity. I said, *your will, not mine.*

And he answered.

But not with a yes from a publisher (not yet anyway). I received peace. And though it wasn't what I asked for, it was the perfectly satiating blessing I hadn't thought to ask for. It was exactly what I needed. Of course it was. God knows what we need. He always does.

He knows precisely what you need too. Seek him and you will find him. You will find answers. You will find peace, you will find encouragement, you will find a friend, and you will find joy or calm or quiet or rest.

> God knows what we need. He always does.

Now, on the contrary, sometimes you may get exactly what you're asking for. Remember when you begged God for that front-row parking spot while running late to church and, voilà, there it was? (You're either rolling your eyes right about now at my trivial prayer or we just became best friends.) How about the illness you prayed away, and it vanished just in time for your anniversary getaway or whatever big plans were on the horizon? Something like that ring a bell?

Or on another twisted side, things may get worse before you see the good or any answer at all. You pray for healing, and you get sicker. And someone else falls ill with the same ole bug. And something else, and someone else. Even so, you know God answers as he sees fit.

So, you invest in rich conversation with the master of all things, asking him to shine through your struggle. And once again, he answers. But (scene from my recent experience), not necessarily with restored health. Instead, he extends the sweetest lowest-key time away you've ever spent with your hubby. Movies, takeout, and reading against the backdrop of the ocean waves. A slow pace that you hadn't planned, but God knew would bless your marriage and make more memories than the action-packed agenda your healthy self had planned. Yes. All things work together for the good. You know this. Don't forget it.

Just keep in mind, many times you may not see the answer as soon as your seeking heart reaches out. Or it may come in a different form. Or maybe, as I have become familiar with, God wants you to call in reinforcements.

> Many times you may not see the answer as soon as your seeking heart reaches out. Or it may come in a different form.

Power in Numbers

I found the sweet fragrance of peace when I pleaded with God through my discouragement three months into my wait for a yes from a publisher. But the story didn't end there, obviously. And the harmonious mood was as fleeting as my successful attempt to avoid my phone first thing in the morning. We need God's help over and over. But his help shows up in colors of all kinds. Maybe my most favorite of his choice of forms to help is his use of his people.

Like little angels, they show up. I swear, I've begged God for help so often I'm surely running out of asks (never). But I've yet to see him poof down from heaven in bodily form into my bedroom like a genie, start folding laundry and begin knocking out my task list. Please let me know if you have. This would make a great story.

What *has* happened. I've prayed for help, and the next day received a text from a friend asking how she can pray for me or offering to run carpool, freeing me to breathe on a desperate-for-a-breath kind of day. Answered prayer.

But reinforcements. We need them. If you're like me, asking for help is one of the hardest things for you to do. It's painful, really. You're not weak, but they'll think you are. Right? Or worse, you'll start to believe you are. Please don't be as foolish as me. Ask for help. But ask for prayer too.

Embarrassing confession. I was probably in the second grade when I became annoyed with little Sally in my Sunday school class rambling on and on about her neighbor's sick cat or cousin's best friend's sore toe. Okay, I don't really remember exactly what so-and-so was asking for prayer for; all I know is that I thought God surely had bigger fish to fry, and this nonsense was wasting his precious time. I have no clue where I got this rationale, but it followed me, and it's messed up.

Me. I'm the messed-up one. Because I was wrong. If it matters to you, it matters to God. It's called perfect love. He's got it for us all. So, it mattered then, and whatever it is on your mind that you're too proud to say or too proud to ask for prayer for, it matters. He listens to all of it, remember. Plus, you'll find most prayer warriors don't play prayer comparison as my elementary school self did. Try them. They are good people.

> ## If it matters to you, it matters to God.

Now, back to little angels and fleeting peace. I decided (or God nudged and prompted me) to surrender and ask for prayer. I found peace when I prayed for a publisher, and all I wanted was that placid peace back. The richness of knowing everything is going to be A-okay. That God has the greatest, most incredible plan unfolding right in front of me. The calmness and confidence that he has my whole world in his mighty good hands and can use my current circumstances just as they are, for his great glory.

I asked anyone who was willing to pray for my peace. Humbly. I didn't compare it to the audacious prayer of a friend battling cancer, and I didn't lift it above the simple prayer of a ten-year-old praying for a sibling with a cold. I saw my personal prayer as a care of the Lord's. And I was received by his people with such grace and love. *Answered prayer.*

And more peace began to unfold. *Answered prayer.*

As I continued to seek God, I continued to see God. As I asked for more prayer, and asked how I could return the favor, I began to see God more. *More answered prayer.*

> **As I continued to seek God, I continued to see God.**

With All Your Heart

One of the most important few words in our focus passage in Jeremiah 29 is found at the end of verse 13: with all your heart.

> You will seek me and find me when you seek me with all your heart. (Jer. 29:13)

We've expanded on the goal to pray without ceasing and what holds us back. We walked through how God listens and the forms of prayer he's listening to. All of them. And we celebrated how he answers. Always. But if you can remember one thing from this chapter about the concept of praying to sum up all the other ideas to help you win over worry, remember this. *With all your heart.* Remember that when it comes to your stubborn worry, anxious thoughts, or feisty fears, it means more. With all you've got. All your heart. When you need more work, more help, more strength, more peace. You've got more work to do.

Pray more. With all your heart. The more your heart seeks, the more your heart will find. The more you take it to God, again and again and again, over and over and over, the more you will find answered prayer.

And the more you will find freedom from your worries.

REFLECTION QUESTIONS

1. Where do you fall on a praying nonstop scale? (1 none, 10 nonstop) How about the frequency of giving him your first fruits? (1 never, 10 daily) Justify.

2. What changes can you incorporate to help you talk to God more? What do you think would change?

3. Do you believe God always listens to your worries and prayers? Describe a time (or times) when you have felt he was listening.

4. Do you expect God to answer your requests with what you want? Think of a time God answered with something different from your request, and then thank him for the good he worked or will work from it.

FIVE

UNSHACKLE IT

Releasing Control

You are not in control.

Repeat note to self: You are *not* in control. Never have been. Never really will be.

God is. Period.

Do you know this? I think we ought to talk it out, because the truth of the matter is, most of us don't live like we really, truly believe it. We run our busy bodies wild and think our thinkers into a tizzy in an attempt to maintain or gain control of just about everything. I do it. You do it. Every single person that walks this weary world does it.

Now, don't get all defensive on me just yet. Maybe, just maybe, I'm not talking to you. You could be thinking, *I'm not a control hog. I'm more of a diligent planner, a thoughtful analytic. I like to be prepared and punctual. It's a good thing.* A-a-ahh . . . I spy a bright red flag, my friend. Let's take a deeper peek and see if you ever tip the scales a bit past diligence into the control zone.

Ponder these hypothetical (or potentially personal—I'll let you decide) scenarios with me. You might have a bent toward controlling if . . .

1. You have prepared a scrumptious meal and your dinner guests are running late. You freak out and obsess over how to preserve your precious goodness to ensure their delight to taste buds. You get all huffy and puffy, venting that they are never on time.

2. You're a germaphobe. Or to put it lightly, you like to call yourself "safe." You triple-mask in well visits to the doctor, have hand sanitizer hidden in every room of your house, won't touch dips at parties (there's always a double dipper lurking), and you've been known to correct others on proper sneezing and hand-washing techniques.

3. You harp on your husband to slow to a near thirty miles per hour hydroplaning-safe speed in the far-right lane on the interstate when it starts to sprinkle. I'll go ahead and fess up to this one. (Get a grip, right?)

4. You took over your kindergartener's Thanksgiving project because you knew she'd make an absolute mess of it. And you're still proofing your sweet baby's (now in high school) homework so she's sure to never miss the A. And now that your children are all grown, you can't help but incessantly slip them directions to whatever is their local destination. (Um, hello, the younger generation can use GPS way better than you can.)

5. Your kid should have had more playing time in the game last night (this isn't the first time you were convinced of this), so you furiously draft your words of appeal and plot your approach to the clueless coach. And you proceed to rant about it with your spouse until you get the nerve to pounce.

6. You're way too busy at work, home, and church, but the job at hand must be done by you, because ain't no one else going to get it done quite right.

7. Or how about this one. You check the weather radar every day leading up to the big event. Or any event. Every ten minutes the morning of. Email any potential person in charge for a backup plan "if." I mean, you've got to get on with your alternative plans for the evening. You stress and stress and stress while waiting for a decision to be made. Refresh, refresh, refresh. Peeking outside for indicators of increased wind speed or change in cloud direction.

8. You tell it. You contend to control people's opinions, thoughts, decisions, their faith. Grapple for authority over your health, safety, success, or that of others. Chase the command of plans, agendas, calendars, and conditions. Vacations. Work meetings. Your appearance, diet, order of your home. On and on. Seeking perfection to create perfection. To avoid the worry-filled what-ifs, looming losses, and potential pains. Control, control, control. Scheming to manipulate situations, obsessing over what might happen, and fighting like heck to control something, someone, some whatever. Something you should've, could've been enjoying, but were too busy thinking yourself into a conundrum about out-of-your-control hogwash.

You hear how silly all that sounds, don't you? Many of my examples are extreme, some slightly embellished. But I bet somewhere through your browse of each, something clicked or connected. Striking a chord of, "Oh yeah, I'm kind of guilty of vying for domination here and there, or sometimes everywhere." Yes, we all have a degree of control-seeking simmering in us.

Who's Really in Control?

Okay, now let's switch gears. Have any of the following ever occurred to you? Listen closely as I push back on some of the pictures painted with realities that clue us in to our actual lack of control in our overanalytical preparation style of behavior. Our lack of control in our life period. Pointing to the truth. The true source of *actual* control: God's almighty sovereignty.

> The true source of *actual* control:
> God's almighty sovereignty.

For starters, scenario number one. Yeah, I'll claim it, I've been this girl and know this helpless soul. It could be: (1) No matter how hot or cold your dish, your sister-in-law is never going to like your chicken tetrazzini. (2) She may be having a bad day, and even her favorite ice cream wouldn't delight her senses. (3) She hasn't eaten in twenty-four hours, and every bite that crosses her palate will taste out of this world. (4) She's getting over a cold, her flavor sensors are numb, and she will tell you it's good no matter what. Or, (5) she was never one to praise the cook, and you won't ever know the truth.

My point is that the possibilities are endless. You are wearing yourself out with all this malarkey. For heaven's sake, enjoy your guest, enjoy yourself, enjoy your life! Give people some grace, and hand yourself a dose while you're at it. Controlling, manipulating, and ruminating is no fun for anyone. You're trying to analyze, prepare, and govern something completely out of your control. If God wants you to receive an award for your best entrée, you'll get it! Some way, somehow. Not by your doing. If it's not what he has in mind for you, he's got his reasons and there's nothing you can do about it. Relax. Move on. It's in his hands. Not yours.

The same goes for everything. All the things. I could keep hammering out every reason you aren't in control of the other thought-consuming matters, but this chapter could get a little too wordy. So, I'll nail down the fact that illness, sickness, germs—God's in control. If he wants you well, he'll protect you even if you lick the plate of your sick kid. If he decides to allow you to succumb to the flu or worse, he'll make sure to jump a germ through your N95 mask. His control. Same goes for regulating your husband's driving. Ahem, Keri. Jesus actually has the wheel, Miss Forgetful. (Though I tend to think Jesus would drive 35 in a downpour.) But only God dominates the weather, your alternative plans (better in the long run), your kid's smarts or success (or lack thereof), your work, and people's opinions of you. Yep, all of that!

When we worry, we are subconsciously creating, preparing for, or predicting future hypothetical scenarios in our minds that are 100 percent out of our rule. And many times, from this anxious mindset, we begin to assume control. I'll be really clear: the enemy is giddy over this shift. He longs for you to think you have control. He loves how crazy you get conceiving and scheming to perfect your life and relying on the unreliable you. It delights him so watching you put your faith in yourself. The last thing he wants is to catch us putting our faith in God.

> When we worry, we are subconsciously creating, preparing for, or predicting future hypothetical scenarios in our minds that are 100 percent out of our rule.

But this is exactly what we should be doing. In our fear and worry, casting every ounce of our fleeting faith where it belongs and can be trusted, in him. Alone. Not in us. I believe somewhere within we know this and find evidence when focused on the infallibility of God's sovereign goodness and dominion. And we uncover further confirmation in our encounters with peace as the litter of our life dissolves in confidence of this gracious truth. But, when we're struck with unknowns and presume control is ours, and then act on it, we are transferring our trust in him to the unreliable *us*. And that is when worrisome thoughts mature and multiply. We seek control because of our worry, and we worry as we seek control. Head spin!

So how about you? Do you believe with all your heart that God is ultimately in control? I think the disconnect lies in the influence of the world's whisper of "you got this" and "if it's to be, it's up to me." Our human forgetfulness of God's authority and our autopilot robotic responses take charge with an overpowering false notion reflecting the chime of culture that we are solely responsible for what happens to us and around us.

Release the Sin of Worry

Well, what do we do about this? This control that's not rightly ours that we are desperately latching onto. I mean, let's be honest, we don't handle the weight of control very well anyway. It's heavy. Knock-down-drag-out exhausting. And we don't really want that. So, how do we live once and for all as if we believe God is in control? How can we surrender ourselves? Unshackle the chains of our own unreliable control. And surrender to him? As worriers trying to unlearn worry (who have apparently been holding a tight grip on control), how do we loosen the noose and release such a restraint?

In Chapter One we recited, "*unlearning* equals *retracing* plus *replacing*." But I'd say we need one more factor. Unlearning worry (and the byproduct *control* in this case) = Retracing + RELEASING + Replacing.

Releasing worry. Releasing fear. Releasing control.

This doesn't mean do nothing. But it does mean surrender your own will, and don't do anything God doesn't nudge or instruct you toward. I bet if you were to ask him (as you should), you certainly wouldn't get an audible "Go ahead and scurry around all unsettled and uneasy, meticulously managing and changing every bit of the life I've placed before you." No, it would sound more like "Be still, release, ease up, rest your restless heart, settle your soul. Know that I've got this." Know that when you seek him wholeheartedly, God, with all his power, will handle what has you rattled and shaken, or will clearly guide, empower, and dress you in his strength to move calmly forward.

What is that deep-rooted fear you have been stewing on? What are the worries simmering at the surface of your thoughts? What are you trying to control, with anxious living, assertive avoidance, overanalyzing, nervous obsession? What do you need to release?

Keep releasing.

Let me step to the side of the path and ask what you know about *repentance*. You may wonder why I'd even pose such a question in the midst of a discussion on control, surrender, and release. But repentance has something to do with *releasing* sin. And believe it or not, *sin*, mine and yours, is all wrapped up in our *worry* and pursuit of control whether we can blatantly distinguish it or not.

It might be broad-as-daylight obvious, like your bold-faced sin-stained lie to cover up words you swear you didn't leak about another mom at the kids' school. (In which case worry about repercussions led to the sin of lying to control.) Or more subtly speaking, the sin could show up in something like cryptic semi-cruel-hearted messaging through your latest jab on social media, in an attempt to control and manipulate the thoughts of your best friend who hopefully scrolls onto your outburst and shifts her reasoning to your liking.

> We don't realize the vast extent of sinful action we take based on our underlying worry in efforts to shift the cosmos, out of fear of what might be.

Consider other take-matters-into-your-own-hands sin committed through deceiving, sneaking, dissing or defaming someone, or something similar, due to dread of what possibly won't go according to your plan. We don't realize the vast extent of sinful action we take based on our underlying worry in efforts to shift the cosmos, out of fear of what might be.

Fear in itself is not a sin. But believing the fear, the lies of the enemy, and taking action based on it definitely leads us to sin. Including the lie that we are in control. We've got to understand that sin is absolutely woven deeply into the threads of our worry and rooted fears. And to truly rid ourselves of the sneaky sin from fear (we want to rid the fibers of our thoughts of worry, don't we?), repentance will be needed.

Repentance. As I uncover the true meaning of this term, it's becoming clearer we can make some serious progress releasing control and freeing ourselves of a little more worry if we better understand repentance and put it into practice.

> To truly rid ourselves of the sneaky sin from fear, repentance will be needed.

Repent and Be Blessed

Merriam-Webster defines the verb *repent* as "to turn from sin and dedicate oneself to the amendment of one's life; to feel regret or contrition."[1] And *repentance* being "the action of repenting"[2] would mean we are talking about the actual action of turning from sin.

Friend, since we are wrong in our belief of the lie of *our* control, and have sinned because of it, repenting comes next to release more worry. By admitting and confessing we have acted on a false

[1]*Merriam-Webster*, s.v. "repent (v)," accessed November 25, 2022, https://www.merriam-webster.com/dictionary/repent.

[2]*Merriam-Webster*, s.v. "repentance (n)," accessed November 25, 2022, https://www.merriam-webster.com/dictionary/repentance.

belief, turning away and accepting we are not in control, and acknowledging that our great God is. Turn from sin. Repent.

I mean, isn't our heart's honest desire to turn hard away from worry? For sure. We're going to delve deeper into how we might do this, but first I want to highlight the benefits of this act to help relay why it's important to learn. (Yep, there's something in it for you!)

How would you like a little *prosperity, purification, forgiveness,* and *refreshment?* Take a second glance at those four words. You want to swallow up some of that, don't you? Maybe one or two more than another, but the Bible has fruitful words to offer about repentance and confession. Now take note. Though similar, confession and repentance are not necessarily the same. Where confession may acknowledge wrong, as does repentance, to *repent* will carry with it remorse. I'll go ahead and assume the best in you, that you have considered some heart change and remorse for what you have become aware is sin in your life. But understand, though confession in general doesn't call for remorse, for the sake of the biblical *confession* references below, know that God is *always* after the heart change. Check out what the Bible has to say about the benefits of such holy gestures.

> People who conceal their sins will not prosper, but
> if they confess and turn from them, they will receive
> mercy. (Prov. 28:13 NLT)

Mercy. Prosperity. I'll take it.

> If we confess our sins, he is faithful and just and
> will forgive us our sins and purify us from all
> unrighteousness. (1 John 1:9)

He will forgive us and purify us. How lovely.

Repent, then, and turn to God, so that your sins may be wiped out, that times of refreshing may come from the Lord. (Acts 3:19)

Times of refreshing. Oh, how I yearn for refreshment.

To *prosper, be purified, forgiven*, and *refreshed*. There are blessings folded in the heart and mission of confession and repentance. Blessings the overwhelmed worrier might be missing. Blessings you may have been missing. Blessings that are no doubt within our reach as a result of the action of repentance.

I've thrown the word "action" around a few times in the past few pages. And for good reason. Though the genuine heart exposes confession to the possibility of repentance, you can't turn from anything without action. We need to create new action. We need to change our actions. Actionable change. Beyond confessing and repenting in our mind, we'll need to also change our outward practices. And to unshackle the weight of worry (derived from our striving to control) for good, *lasting* change is what we are ultimately after.

Accountability

I touched on changes in the last chapter to aid in our effort to pray continually, but I'll come right out and tell you that the most effective way I've found to adopt and hold to anything new is by acquiring accountability. And ironically, confession and accountability more or less go hand in hand. When we confess aloud our shortcomings, a flow of accountability follows, as we often feel an immediate sense of liability to ourselves and to God. But personally, when I'm playing for the sure-bet win of change, I double down for the greater reward by tracking down and nailing into place an additional external barrier. More accountability. The gooey sweet spot change sticks to.

> When we confess aloud our shortcomings, a flow of accountability follows, as we often feel an immediate sense of liability to ourselves and to God.

It's a bit of a doozy. The process of attaining accountability is not so attractive, and quite a turnoff to most. It's uncomfortable to ask for, it forces you to admit you aren't in control (not easy for the controlling worrier), and it comes at the price of work and humility. Scary stuff.

But it's worth it. Think about it. Have you ever put yourself out there, shared a goal with a friend, or even joined someone with the same objective and followed through to success? A new business venture, a new workout plan, a work of words or art? Consider something you opted to do solo but asked for prayer to help you see it through. Or a mission you pursued while teamed up with a buddy. You likely don't have to reflect long to recall the benefits of a partner in crime or a bold friend who held you to your word.

In 2014, I registered as a first-timer for the local mini-marathon before I began training. Before I even knew how to train for a race. I also secretly signed up my husband as a later-to-find-out-not-so-pleasant surprise. Because, hey, I knew an accountability partner would be my best friend in such a quest. Little did I know I'd be his accountability partner. After a few amateur goal-pondering moments, I disclosed to Mike my intention to complete the 13.1 miles three months later in under two hours.

Next box to check, someone with a little more interest in teaming up on my latest ambition. I trickled out the news and came up with two running partners who would pace an average nine miles per hour, about what I needed to meet my random goal.

I accepted the challenge, and we joined forces. Now, I may have had to resist the constant urge to throw up when I ran with those speed demons, but I kept pace. No way was I going to be left in their dust. Speaking of dust, running solo, there'd be none to trail, right? But with the help of bodies rallied next to me, dragging me along, I trained harder. I grew stronger. Ready and conditioned for the race.

Accountability.

Without it, what's your track record? Think New Year's resolutions. Any flops there? Maybe you silently swore you'd eat one less scoop of ice cream each night, but by evening number two you were quick to tell your imaginary accountability partner, "Resolutions are dumb. God made ice cream to enjoy anyway." Plus, she's not even real. No guilt. You're good. God's good. Two scoops of ice cream—good!

What if you'd had accountability? Posted on social media your dessert diet, announced it to the kids, instructed your hubby to leave Cookies & Cream off the grocery list. Gathering your own little army to help you fight? Heaven knows you'll need it. You love nothing more than to slowly savor that hard-earned frozen creamy wholesomeness at the end of a long day. Or mull over whatever your resolution or attempt at change was that went anything like that. Sometimes you've had help, and other times you've kept some resolutions to yourself. Which ones stuck? Which ones became habits?

What we're going for here is new habits to replace the old. And new habits form with repetitive change. And change is just more likely to repeat itself when accountability is present. When someone is checking on you, cheering for you, and watching you and your self-conscious fear of judgment for slipping up. Find someone to join you. Find someone to check up on you.

New habits form with repetitive change.
And change is just more likely to repeat
itself when accountability is present.

Tell your spouse, tell a trusted friend, tell your Bible study, something like, "Sorry to bug you, but I think I've been a bit wrapped up in trying to control the variables of my life. I'm here to say, I know I'm not in control. God is. If you see, hear, or witness anything out of me that appears to reflect otherwise, will you call me out?" I don't know, maybe that sounds a touch weird to you. Be you.

Shoot, blab your confession on Facebook if you feel so compelled. Yeah, I know that might be perceived as a bit showy and annoying to the social police, but if you're serious about turning away from a behavior, you might need to test all the stops. Maybe no one will say a word, or maybe the algorithms will hide your confession. But I bet you'll filter your future content through the lens of the consumers of social media. And you didn't put an end date, so maybe it'll stick.

As for most of you geniuses with zero interest in airing your dirty laundry to the mass media, I get it. I'm over it too. Stick with a person or a group you trust. Or another super choice: counselors or paid professionals are really good at this accountability thing. It pretty much goes with the job description. I know countless people for whom therapy is their go-to. Smart people, with smart advice. Advice on tried, true, and tested action and change designed to help you carry out your specific goal.

It's worked wonders for me too. Well, until life threw too many curveballs, I slacked on my homework, and started to cancel. Not you, though; you'll be ready, and you know change takes work. I'm giving you a heads-up now. You want to win over your worry. So, it may feel easier to bail on your accountability when you're not doing the work or making the changes, especially if you're paying someone and believe yourself to be in the boss's seat. But hang in there. I know it's painful to admit if you slouch and mess up, but we're after humility too, right? Give it your best shot. And at the end of the day, if it just doesn't work for you, I'll give us both some grace. It's your dollar anyway. Your call.

I don't know, maybe a friend you have no intention of unfriending would make a better option. Another idea. Your girls-night-out mom crew? They'll always ask for updates on your latest endeavor. You can count on it. You can count on them. Try them. Or simply that tell-it-like-it-is friend who can't help but dig below the surface to open all your raw wounds. They are the best!

Bottom line. Fess up your anxious, worrying, controlling thoughts to someone. Accountability works. You've now put yourself in the limelight. Everyone or someone's watching. Someone knows you're turning from worry. Someone will catch you real quick in the wrong. And this is good. Like writing this book. My whole wide world knows it's about worry. I put it out there. All over the place. Friends, friends of friends, social media strangers. Dare I expose my worry about trying to control all the sloppy pieces of a book about worry? You better believe I have. Oops! But you better believe I've been called out on it and learned to think twice before I give in to the temptation. Reminder number 999, God's in control. Right. Got it!

> Bottom line. Fess up your anxious, worrying, controlling thoughts to someone. Accountability works.

Will you find someone to be accountable to? Will you stop where you are right now and jot down the name of who it will be? What will you say? If you don't have a soul to spill it to, I'm free! Love to help. Email me. I check it every day. I'll respond as long as the spam filter doesn't block you with some off-the-wall email address. But I'm your girl if you're drawing a blank here. Totally serious. That's how much I want to win this war over worry with you.

God's Will

Did you get distracted with wondering how my mini-marathon story ended ('cause I know I do this)? It sounded like I had good control of my training, wouldn't you say? Well, that race story wasn't intended to be about control or my lack thereof; it was merely to serve as a demonstration of how accountability can assist our efforts to pull off something new (like accountability to kick worry and control from our life). Though the way this story unfolds, interestingly, speaks to our insufficient control.

I trained well. All measures of accountability had me ready to run. On practice race day, I did it. A record nine-minute mile times thirteen. Less than two hours. And all my sources swore the adrenaline at the real event would kill that personal record. Then the cool, heavy with clouds spring day arrived, and I was on course. Eleven miles in and I had twenty minutes to complete the remaining two miles. Plenty of time to meet my goal. The praise music rang louder in my ears. A happy dance in each step. It was happening!

And then. God opened the heavens above. Drops turned to puddles, turned to soggy inches suctioning the soles of my new runners to the thick earth below. My feet became lead weights. My pace slowed. Mile twelve. Calves clenched tight. Solid. I screamed to my brain, "Legs, move!" They inched, crawled. My mind blurred, soaked. I finished. Two hours and twenty seconds.

Twenty seconds. Flop. I missed it.

Who was in control?

I tried. But it wasn't me.

This disappointment wasn't recognized at the time as a lesson about who is in the actual driver's seat of my circumstances. And though I see it clearly now, all that crossed my mind then was failure and "what the heck was all the waste of time of three months of training for?"

But God wasn't done teaching me lessons about his control in my life. He never stops. He is always pursuing us with his plans and his purpose. And later, our Creator allowed the creative lessons in his sovereignty to work out more in my favor.

God's Way

The truth is, I still haven't rediscovered the exact words that changed everything for me, and I can't recall the verbatim phrases as they were written, but I'll never forget the sentiment that cracked open my heart and what I was controlling my way through unsuccessfully, in another phase of life.

Once decided, I spent six months with not a split second lacking a thought of the goal. To conceive one more time and bring forth another child of God into our family. Into this world in need of more faithful children. *Where there's a will, there's a way,* I'd chanted to my hardwired perseverance. But what I once believed to be God's will inched its way through my determination, birthing sheer my-way human will.

I held the reins tight. And tighter. Whipping the rope, shifting the plan, manipulating moments, analyzing the why of each negative test turned one hundred, researching new supplements, new findings. As if God is in the business of saying "have a baby," but really means "learn all you can about obstetrics and gynecology." I controlled. I tried to control. I was out of control. Where I had no control.

> ## God has a plan. His plan. His timing.

I missed life. I missed the blessing of the journey. I worried more. And more. Fear of what might not be. Crippling fear. Something had to give.

It wasn't supposed to be that way. Friends, it's not. God has a plan. His plan. His timing. Maybe a baby was on the horizon for me. But I was trying to force my way, right away. He didn't say go ahead and bring a child into this world and make sure you drive yourself nuts seeing that it happens. Just as he doesn't give us instruction with a timetable on when he'll bring about the fruits of any of our labor. Usually, it's just *obey as I say, and I'll take care of the rest.*

I got the memo. Thank goodness. I wrestled in my own misery for six months first. But, I continued seeking him hard, and the message God started to send my way can be summed up in the reminder that *if it's not God's will, I can't force it, and if it is God's will, there's nothing I can do to stop it* (Acts 5:38–39). I wanted God's will. I hope you do too. I hope you're beginning to understand his will is what's best. It's the sweetness of life. Your best life. And whatever is his true will, you can't stop it. His will always prevails. It's a promise (Prov. 19:21).

> ## His will is what's best.

So, I bought in. If it was God's will for me to have this baby, he'd come through. I chilled out for a bit. I confessed my guilty resolve to control, even surrendered with an open heart to adoption or to whatever his plan would be. Surrendered. To his will, not mine. And lo and behold, four weeks later an extra pink line on that little stick of plastic, the one that still hides in my bathroom drawer five years later, reminded me who's in charge of the very good plan of my life.

How good God is to look out for us. How amazing it is that he is in absolute control. How wonderful that we don't have to carry that weight. How incredible that even if things don't go our way, we can surrender our ways to him and rest assured our future is in his mighty, perfect hands.

Surrender All

Do you trust in God's control? Why wouldn't you, right? He made you, he designed and placed every single strand of hair on your head, and he created the entirety of this big beautiful earth and the infinite universe beyond.

He is in control. You and I are not. When we worry and make strides to control our world, sin creeps in. To eradicate this unwanted stench, we confess and repent, opening the door to God's blessings and good plan. Opening the path of unlearning worry as we release control of our cares to God's ultimate authority and unleash a new life of freedom from fear.

Trust me, we are uber-unreliable when left in full charge of our lives. We have no clue what tomorrow holds and can only spot a sliver of a speck of the big picture of our eternity. Thank God, he is in control—100 percent control. God, help us sink that truth into our worldly warped ways.

When it comes to winning over worry, we've got to release the reins and plow into our stubborn spirit the truth of who has control over where we've been, where we are, and what's coming our way. It's him. It's him. It's him.

In our living and in our dying. God knows how and when he wants to use us, and God knows when he wants us home. Only he knows. Only he calls the shots. Not you, not me, not the enemy who knocks you down. Every day, all day, to the end, it's him. In control.

> **Every day, all day, to the end, it's him. In control.**

He loves you. He can be trusted. You don't need to worry. You don't need to fear. Release, confess, turn away from sin, latch on to accountability. Surrender the old. Surrender control.

Surrender all.

I'm hearing Carrie Underwood's angelic rendition of this perfectly fitting classic melody. Look it up, give her a listen. Sing with your heart with me . . .

I surrender all, I surrender all;
All to Thee, my blessed Savior,
I surrender all.

Friend, hands held high, palms face up, surrender your fear, surrender your worry, surrender your life to the one and only Lord of your life.

He's got you. Always. Forever . . . and *ever*.

REFLECTION QUESTIONS

1. How do you try to control in the face of worry? List as many ways as you can think of.

2. Do you understand that you are not truly in control? Who is, and how do you know?

3. What does your sin look like in your worry and attempt to control?

4. Are you ready to repent, to surrender to God's will and better way? How?

PART TWO

WARRIOR

UNLEASH IT

SIX

UNLEASH YOUR ARMOR
Using Your Warrior Weapons

Do you feel like a warrior?

Personally, my daily tendency is to grumble and groan the moment I make the first attempt to adjust to daylight while resisting the urge to snug up tighter under the covers in safety and security. So, I chuckle in response to this question, because "warrior" is definitely not the first word I would use to describe the raw me. But it's a word I'm beginning to grow into.

How about you? Do you wake up some days wimpy? Or do you greet most days as a warrior? I'm pretty sure that's a "no way, Jose!" To back up this bold assumption, I decided to have some fun and create a small home test case. Here's how it went:

Victim #1—Teenage boy.

Me: "Will, do you feel like a warrior when you get up in the morning?"

Will: An assertive, "HA!! No."

Me: Internal response. *Yep, as expected. Thanks for your honesty.*

Victim #2—Ten-year-old Kaitlyn.

Me: "Kaitlyn, do *you* feel like a warrior?"

Kaitlyn: A casual shrug and meh sort of smirk, "Uh, sometimes."

Me: "Really? Okay!"

Kaitlyn: "Well . . . when I'm at recess and I'm beating all the boys at basketball."

Me: Proud giggle brimming with thoughts of *Love this girl's confidence. Can someone bottle me up some swigs of that?*

Victim #3—Tween daughter.

Me: "Abigail, when your feet first hit the floor in the morning, do you feel like a warrior?"

Abigail: Deer-in-headlights response, "Uhh . . . I don't know. Warrior of what?"

Me: "Just, do you feel like a warrior?"

Abigail: "Sure?" as if "yes" was the answer I was after, "But warrior of what?"

Me: Throwing her a bone, "To face the day?"

Abigail: Now positively sure of one final thought, "I feel tired."

Me: In inner agreement, *Exactly.*

Victim #4—My husband.

Mike: Listening in, preplanning, and ready with his "Umm . . . no. And definitely not before my coffee."

Me: Silent smile and inside dialogue. *I hear that, honey.*

Victim #5—My dad.

I moved along outdoors to the driveway in search of my dad, to find him corralling my two tireless toddlers. God bless him. He's seventy years old, and he's been helping me with the twins a few mornings a week. Maybe I'll get a yes from what I'd say looks a lot like a warrior at the moment.

Me: Sparking conversation sharing a peek at my day's writing focus—I can't get enough of his unfailing interest in my latest piece—I abruptly interrupted with, "Dad, do you feel like a warrior when you get up?"

Dad: Chuckled out a "*Pffft!* . . . Never."

Me to self: *Even my hero, my dad, in all his experience and godly wisdom admitted he doesn't wake up a warrior.*

I think we can stop here. Probably no need to run around the rest of the block. The truth is, I doubt many honest folks would claim they feel like a warrior. Especially before they gear up with armor for the day. (Or shots of caffeine, right?)

Now let's say you're one of those special human beings. You bounce to your feet with your "Not today, Satan" shield before the alarm clock startles you from your defenseless sleep. Oh, yes, I see you. You 5:00 a.m. go-getter, sleeping with your sports bra on and running shoes under the nightstand. Topped with your daily devotion bookmarked in advance to today's date. Wedged next to your all-caught-up Bible study, plus "I love Jesus" pencil, multicolored highlighter, and extra sticky notes. Whew. All of it ready to be put to good use as you energetically wake to your auto-coffee brewing a perfect inhale of refreshing aroma, followed by your perfectionistic exhale of "it's going to be a fantastically productive day." You're a waking warrior. Yay, you!

But. I'd put the hundred bucks (I really don't have) in my purse on the fact that maybe you are a lot like me. Let's see what you think.

It looks like this: I didn't get to bed quite as early as I hoped last night—again. Which means I snooze at least once, probably don't fall back asleep because I have reached "that age," and am slapped with the realization it's not the weekend and I actually have to get stuff done. And I don't want to. I'm tired, and I'm weak. But nonetheless, I thank God for the day. And because I've learned that this intentional spiritual shift in mindset helps me fight the strong pull back under the sheets. And refocus more toward his warrior thinking. I'm not quite throwing on an indestructible "Not today, Satan" shield, but it's enough to drag my feet to the floor, push open the shutters, and whisper a hopeful "Hello" to the day.

So, I get it. We don't all wake up feeling like warriors. The weight you're trying to carry into a given day can be intense, or you may never feel like a warrior. A worrier, yes! Got that down. A warrior? Sounds great, but how?

So glad you asked. We've worked the past five chapters on the first half of unlearning worry by *retracing*. Up next, *replacing*. Basically, we've been retracing, rehashing, and dismantling our old faulty worrier beliefs and thought patterns with the hope of replacing it all. And here we are. Ready to swap out the unreliable, unsound rubbish with trustworthy warrior weapons to shield us from the lies of fear. To sustain us as the conquerors we are in and through Christ. We've gathered an understanding and unraveled the worries we dug up from our past and present. We uncovered the ugly face of the true enemy. We unloaded our burdens in deepened prayer. And finally unshackled the control, which never belonged to us in the first place, through surrender and repentance.

Four Fear Filters

It's time to face the world with a new lens where worry is faint and our faith is wildly big and bold. Time to add in more robust weapons, tenacious tools, and bulletproof armor. Time to solidify and trust in God's trustworthy truths.

But, in order to *trust* the truths, we have to *believe* the truth, right? Since we've long since been manipulated and learned over decades to believe lies, we've got to adopt a fresh new lens to look through, to filter out the false. And the fears. A God-sized filter that will unleash a shiny crystal clear view and belief in what is real and what is true. It's this renewed godly focus we must determine to choose every single morning. A focal point that will open the doorway of filtering out fear and disintegrating worry down to dust in the face of our unshakable belief in the truth.

Belief in the truth is your greatest weapon against worry. I want to remind you that I had to learn this stuff too. I still am. And I get pretty pumped to share these perspectives with you because I absolutely need the refresher myself. Remember, I don't wake up a natural-born warrior either. Yep, Satan is round the clock on my heels—that snake!

> ### Belief in the truth is your greatest weapon against worry.

So, let's talk more about the lenses we need to strap on our focus each day to turn our inner *worrier* into *warrior*. These magnifiers of faith that filter out fear I've labeled our "Four Fear Filters." You have to understand, these filters and strategies, when I don't neglect to use them, sit my wretched worry and fear in time-out, where they stay until I say they can get up. They really do work.

The first is the biggest doozy of a winner. Here it goes:

Filter of God's Word

There is nothing more powerful than God's words. The Bible has nearly eight hundred thousand of them. That's a hefty lot of bullets to fight the enemy with, wouldn't you say? But here's the problem. Not even Einstein could remember eight hundred thousand words at once.

We identified two underlying fears at the root of our worries, but just like all forms of herbicide won't kill all varieties of weeds, it helps to load up with the appropriate words from God to best tackle each particular fear.

Remember our Foundation Fibs (the lies of Satan we have been believing), *I am helpless* and *I am worthless*. More importantly, do you remember the Trusted Truths, *I have help* and *I am worthy*? These two truths need their scriptural counterparts to strengthen their blow against the lies. To do this, we need to memorize these words in God terms. And here's why. You have help and worth because of him. It has nothing to do with your personal power. It has everything to do with his. His power. And his love.

If you start thinking for a second that it's in your mind-over-matter power to beat down your worrisome thoughts, that's the moment you lose ground and fear takes charge. In God terms, we should say: I always have help because God is all-powerful. And I am infinitely worthy because God's love is perfect. These are your fighting truths backed by an army of eight hundred thousand supporting words. And you, my warrior friend, have all of them at your fortunate fingertips.

> I always have help because God is all-powerful.
> And I am infinitely worthy because
> God's love is perfect.

Have you ever scurried straight to God's Word or asked him what he thinks about your "worry of the day" or "fear of the season" as soon as the unease surrounds you? Maybe you're not super familiar with his words or what he'd say, but if you do have some experience with his messages, I'd love to encourage you to consider them in the face of your fear.

If you'd just pause and ask him what he thinks about your finances, family, emotional or health concerns (whatever has you worked up in worry), you might be surprised when verses fly to the front of your thinking and shake off some sweat and angst.

But, even if you find yourself staring at a blinking cursor, a blank canvas, or have never loaded up with more of his mighty words, will you seek them out with me? You can borrow a few of mine for now that back up the Trusted Truths, but no kidding, there's some incredibly impressive stuff in the Bible. Flip through it and arm yourself with me.

Truth #1: God is all-powerful. He holds all power. (Col. 1:16, Luke 1:37). He created all things and has power over all of it. Every speck of it, my friend. This means there's nothing he can't do. That helplessness you feel—God's got you covered. He can and will provide. He is in control. And, one more time, has All. The. Power—over all things.

A question one might ask here is, "But, how do I know his provision will be good? So okay, he can do all things, but what if what he does with his power is not what I want? He may not care what I want. How can I trust he'll provide and protect in a way that's suitable for me and my life?" Valid thought. If. If we didn't know the extent of God's character and promises. It's true, he can and does do what he sees fit, and it may not always be what you want. This is where the next truth swoops in and saves the day.

Truth #2: God's love is perfect. His love for you is perfect. Without fault, it fully fills, and is single-handedly sufficient (1 John 4:16–17). And because nothing can separate us from God's love (Rom. 8:38–40), God's perfect love is absolutely unconditional. And perfect love cares. This means we can be crazy confident that he most surely does care about what you care about. He feels when you feel. He cries when you cry. You may not see it. You may not always get what you think you need, and so wonder if you're not seen, but he certainly sees. In fact, God sees what you don't. He's got the big picture in view. He sees it, he wrote it.

His love is unconditional. In case you need clarification, yes, that means without any conditions. And I can't help but repeat, nothing can separate you from that love. So, when it comes to those feelings and fears of worthlessness, this perfect love makes your value purely priceless to your Creator. Thus, your worth is not up for debate. Not with your mother-in-law, your ex, your used-to-be bestie, your mama's new husband. Whoever!

> God's perfect love is absolutely unconditional.

"There is no fear in love, but perfect love casts out fear" (1 John 4:18 ESV). Casts out fear—what?! Yes, you read right. Can you wrap your arms around this best news ever? Perfect love, which you have access to, can cast out, knock out, whisk away, make go away. All fear. If you can learn to believe the truth that God's love is perfect, and that he loves you unconditionally, which means he's got your best interest at heart. And combine that trustworthy good care of you with the truth that he is powerful enough to do *all* things. Then what in the world do you have to fear? Nothing, right? This is why this scripture is wildly important to tattoo onto the walls of your heart and your sturdiest, strongest beliefs. If you really, really could get this. Like deep, deep down in the crevices of your sunken soul. Your fear and worry would shrivel up so fast you'd forget you had an enemy hot after you.

I want you to understand that the "Filter of God's Word" is this. Scripture. And you need these words that are 100 percent reliable and trustworthy. God-breathed words. Read them, write them, paint them on the wall, and frame them. The key objective is to hunt them down and soak them in. Lock in God's truths until they slip quickly from your tongue and become your first line of defense when worry strikes and startles. You need to see them everywhere.

I've been known to invest in the necessary armor of visuals in my home. The "It Is Well" plaque on my dresser, the "Be Still" hand-carved wooden script beside my bedroom door, and the "God Is Mightier than" Psalm 93:4 sign resting in front of my computer in my peripheral view. These trinkets, tokens, and reminders all serve as constant "God filters," shifting my subconscious focus to fear-fighting truth throughout each day. They help.

But let's say you haven't yet plastered declarations throughout the halls of your home to remind you to constantly filter your worry through God's words. In that case, I've got a task for you right now. Hold this spot mid-paragraph, grab the closest pen (go ahead), and scribble on a sticky note or scrap paper a fear-fighting verse that speaks to you. Or simply jot down these truths: "God Is All-Powerful" and "God's Love is Perfect." Use it as a bookmark through the remainder of these pages while committing to memory the truths that will filter out worry and fear.

Did you do it yet?

When the tiniest worry jostles your thoughts, or oversized fear overwhelms your soul, declare with every fiber of your faith that (1) God is all-powerful, and there is nothing that will leave you helpless in his presence. Nothing. And (2) God's love is perfect, so no matter what tempts you with feelings of worthlessness, you are covered sufficiently and unconditionally. You are valued, prized, and loved more than you could possibly imagine.

Filter of God's People

It's certainly obvious all the way back to the beginning of Genesis how God used his people to portray his good character and promises. And though millions of moons have circled since, God is still in the business of using everyday people to witness to you and me. People who can serve as great defenses and weapons in your war on worry. Can I encourage you to seek them out? This is huge.

Pastors for one. Go to a church that preaches the whole of the Holy Bible. Their calling and captivating convictions have the potential to light a blazing fire in you for God's goodness and power. And if something is keeping you from church, God has another brilliant solution for those of us lucky enough to make it to the twenty-first century. Online services. Thank God for that! Needing a pep talk about worry and fear? You might just find it there!

Books. You're reading this one now, congratulations! But would you believe I'm not the first writer to write about worry and fear? (Insert sarcasm and a wink.) Here's one for you, *Fierce Faith*, by my friend and coach Alli Worthington, God love her. Well-written book, friend-to-all author, and an excellent source to keep your perspective on faith over fear.

> God is still in the business of using everyday people to witness to you and me.

And Joyce Meyer. Wise, funny friend Joyce. Her book *Unshakeable Trust* whipped me into shape and woke me up. Knowing tireless trust is something I needed a ton more of to knock out my nagging worry, the title alone made me have to have it. Plus, she apparently gets oodles of inspired words from God to pass on to struggling souls like me—evident from over a hundred published books. Rub off some of that wisdom my way, please.

Seriously, just Google Christian "worry" and "fear" books, and *bam*, you've got godly perspectives for days and years to beef up your fight.

Or, maybe you prefer podcasts, following a Scripture-posting Christian on social media, or subscribing to encouraging recurring devotions focused on fueling your faith. Oh yeah, I have one. Shameless plug. (Wink again!)

But here's the point of all this. There are fired-up-for-Jesus people all over the place who can't keep their mouths shut on behalf of the Holy Spirit. Stirred-up spiritual souls who want nothing more than to share perspectives to help you filter your fear-scuffed thoughts through. Filters of faith that fight the lies of worry and fear by shifting your focus to the truth of God's power and love. Seek them out, read their words, listen to their voices. Let them help fill you with God's Word and give you armor and shield you from the enemy.

Filter of Your Own Advice
You might find yourself on the fence here. *My own advice, really? If I had good advice to give about my worry, I wouldn't be halfway through this book. I'd be living my great advice, and voilà— worry gone!*

But I have a feeling about you. I believe you do have good advice to lend. Think about it. Has a friend ever come to you with a struggle? Seeking aid in a decision that she was naturally a bit anxious or worried about? Unsure how to handle the concern? And did she ask your opinion? I bet, yes! And you've been delighted to rattle off, maybe even proud of, your insight too, huh? I mean, you might have later thought "easier said than done." But still, as far as her sticky situation, you felt pretty confident in the blooming wisdom you've likely gained from your own personal experience. You were happy to share your advice.

The truth is, many times we do have some effective strategies to handle problems. But, when our own situation gets all twisted up in our own minds with Satan's schemes to confuse, cast doubt and fear, we become lost and lose clarity.

So, turn it around. Imagine a friend came to you with your exact same worry and fear. What would you tell her (tell yourself)? This may sound super simple and even juvenile, but sometimes it's just the kick in the pants we need to shift perspective. Tune in to my coffee date last week with one of my dearest, most godly friends, Sarah.

• •

Sarah: "I have been torn up lately about how well my kids are being spiritually fed."

Me: "Oh yes, I've *sooo* been there! Tell me more."

Sarah: "I wonder (worry) if I'm presenting God's Word to them enough, teaching them to serve well, allowing adequate exposure to Christian friendships, sufficiently modeling faithful behaviors, or even attending the right church to feed and encourage their spiritual growth."

Me: "Oh, Sarah, I know these voices all too well. (Don't we all?) But I assure you, you are doing a wonderful job. And besides, we give ourselves way too much credit. God has their hearts. I think it's commendable you're thinking about this and praying over it. I know

God hears you. And he will surely help open doors to minister to their hearts. But at the end of the day, they are his. He has a plan for them. And we can't control every detail."

••

Okay, all that was easy for me to say, right? Because I'm not in Sarah's shoes. But guess what? I 100 percent have stood in Sarah's shoes. Many times. And I know Sarah. She'd speak the exact same wise words to me. But yet, she can't see the truth in her own struggle. You know one reason why? Because Satan is messing with her. He's heckling her on her issues and tormenting me on mine.

He is confusing Sarah with cracked contemplation, webs of worrisome thoughts, and lies. He hungers for her exhaustion over the demands of the Christian mom life. Here's what he for a fact does not want. Her to be confident in her diligence to keep pursuing ways to bring God to her children. And he definitely doesn't want her to have any peace about any portion of it.

When Sarah faces her fear with the truth that God is *all-powerful* and has the same *perfect love* for her kids that he does for her, her worries start to scatter in the wind of joy and calm. It is there that she enjoys more of the calling on her life to walk five of God's children through the world, exponentially multiplying the Christian population. And that's the last thing Satan wants. So, he forges on firmer, harder to deceive Sarah.

But since Satan wasn't messing with or tricking me with that matter at the moment, I could see the truth more clearly over my friend's struggle. Well, it's time to trick him back. Flip your fear around and insert your own advice. And do it up front. It can serve as a mighty weapon against worry. When you know you'd tell a friend not to worry or would give a good pal a pass to dismiss the lies of fear, swivel around and share the same message with yourself.

Flip your fear around and insert your own
advice. And do it up front. It can serve
as a mighty weapon against worry.

Filter of Your Worst-Case Scenario

Now, this last one may sound a little backwards, but working through the worst-case scenario with my worry really has been a game changer. First, let me give you the encouraging truth of applying such a lens and perspective shift. The majority of the time, the worst-case scenarios we dread never take place. It's true. Though the hard reality, on the occasional other side of the equation, is that the worst-case scenarios do manifest in our for-real life or in the life of someone we love. Sometimes.

But, more often than not, we're dealing with false worst-case *what-ifs* sneaking into our "worrier" subconscious, parading around in our mind until they sizzle and swell into our darkest gut-wrenching fears. We wind up envisioning our ultimate devastation in a daymare, where the unimaginable becomes imaginable. But there's a huge piece always missing from this very unlikely scene.

Yep, you guessed it. God. We tend to follow a rabbit trail with our thoughts to a spiral of horror that is not only false because we've made the whole thing up, but also not even possible because we're missing the truth that God will be there along with his power and love. You can count on it.

Why do we neglect that major piece? I'll tell you. The liar and trickster, for one. Satan is secretly concealing that very crucial portion of the big picture. He was certainly playing this game with me. So, I started stopping the story. As soon as I enter the climax of the drama, where my stomach flip-flops around like a fish on land that can't catch a breath, I strike back at the snake. I shake my flustered brain and force all my horrid thoughts to a prettier place. Distracting, diverting, or doing whatever is necessary to exterminate the sting of my fear.

> The majority of the time, the worst-case scenarios we dread never take place.

But there's another way to handle these daymares.

Play it out. Don't stop it.

Yep, you heard me right. Keep going down that dark path. But then add the truth at the end. Place God in the picture and keep him there. He's there anyway. But now, I want you to truly see him there. Picture his unconditional perfect love. Feel it. Acknowledge his mighty power to provide. Know it's real. Let it console and enfold you. Hear him say he's got you. Hear him tell you he has everyone surrounding you in his good care too. God won't be gone for a split second. He will be working around the clock, even when you don't see it, to work out all your troubles. For your good.

> And we know that in all things God works for the good of those who love him, who have been called according to his purpose. (Rom. 8:28)

> God won't be gone for a split second. He will be working around the clock, even when you don't see it, to work out all your troubles. For your good.

Hard to admit this, but I'll tell you why I never, previous to my revelation, included God in my worst-case scenario. You may think this is absurd, or who knows, maybe this is you too. For example, say I let my wandering thoughts take me to a hypothetical dreaded place, such as one of my children's funerals (God forbid, but this was the real of my mind). If I parked my thoughts in the depth of such dread and admitted that I knew without a shadow of a doubt that God would be with me, accepting I could somehow by his grace survive the trauma, then I thought this admission would shift God's plans and thoughts to: "Oh, okay. Keri can handle this assignment. I'll let her have that one!" To which I would plead, "I didn't mean it! No, I cannot handle that. So, you'll give it to one of your stronger servants, right? Okay, thanks!"

There is so much wrong with this entire dialogue. The truth is, we can't manipulate God's mind. His plans for us aren't rash, rushed, or random. Our plans are in God's good hands—period. Not mine, not yours. He decides. Anyway, he knows what you can and can't handle well before you do. Before you even existed. In fact, not a single soul can handle it without him. Or handle anything. And the fabulous news is, we don't ever have to.

> Our plans are in God's good hands—period.
> Not mine, not yours. He decides.

You may as well go ahead and put him smack-dab in the middle of the moment as you entertain your dark daymares. Because the true reality is, the revised worst-case scenario acknowledging the truth of God's presence adds a whole heck of a lot more peace. Yes, peace please. Which is way better than your prior "worst case." Amen? Not to mention, nothing you think will change what he has already planned and prepared. Nothing you say will shift what he has purposed and ordained. And well before you were even woven together in your mother's womb. True. And true.

Take that for a fear-fighting filter!

You Are a Warrior

These are no doubt some fierce fear filters if you hang on to them. Grabbing a hold of unrelenting worry and jabbing it with declarations of God's actual words and promises. Strengthening your stance with the convictions of other Christians. Sucker punching the lies with your own retrospective advice. Arming yourself with the absolute truth that even if you are thrown off course with the unwanted, undesirable scenario coming to pass, you can rise up and move on with more peace. Bottom line, fear will not totally take you out because God is always, always there holding your hand.

> Though he may stumble, he will not fall, for the LORD upholds him with his hand. (Ps. 37:24)

So, do you feel like a warrior?

Well, I get it. Most of the time, no. Break of day, before we throw on our armor, we don't wake with an automatic warrior badge. But did any of these filters resonate with you or give you a hint of hope? I promise you, within these lenses lie our unwavering warrior weapons.

Find a verse that fuels your feisty fight. Tell yourself your Christ-centered soul knows better and would say, "God's got you. And he's got this." Hoist that "Not today, Satan" shield and fire back at the enemy with the truth. The indisputable trustworthy truth that no matter what comes your way today, God is with you, and nothing can or ever will take that away. No tragedy, no sorrow, no disappointment, and no mountain will ever be too big for God to run through, lift up, climb over, swallow up and conquer. Nothing.

> As for God, his way is perfect: The LORD's word is flawless; he shields all who take refuge in him. (Ps. 18:30)

It is God who arms me with strength and keeps my way secure. (Ps. 18:32)

His strength is with you. Wherever you go. So, though you may not feel like a warrior when you're weak and weary, he's there. His hands never cease to stretch out, to open wide. Ready, waiting to load you down with weapons that block out and knock out your fear. Because of his fullness of power surrounding you, and his perfect love within you, you are indeed a warrior, my friend. You are a well-equipped warrior with all the right weapons to win your war over worry.

It's time to unleash your armor!

REFLECTION QUESTIONS

1. Do you feel like a warrior? What lenses and armor do you put on to filter out fear as you approach your day?

2. What words from God can you commit to memory to fight the fear of helplessness and worthlessness?

3. How can you let God's people help you fight your worry? What advice would you give yourself?

4. Do you fear your worst-case scenario coming to be? What would change if you truly accepted the truth of God's presence, power, and perfect love in all your worries?

SEVEN

UNLEASH YOUR PEACE
Fighting Off Life's Storms

One hundred thirty-six streak-free square panes stretch wall to wood-planked wall. Floor to twenty-foot vaulted ceiling directly before me. It's crystal clear flawless. Rich shades of spring Kentucky green bouncing off every limber limb, elegantly, gracefully draping over the serene sprawling view of Lake Herrington. The leaves dance. The sun peeks in and out of bright white clouds touching the surface of the water. It sparkles.

The dock below warmly invites with its plush chaise lounges and sectional sofa. And maybe I'll traipse down the staircase later, but for now I couldn't be more content. It's quiet and cool inside. The cream-colored cushions and plump pillows embracing my recline. My eyes scan the room. The brand-new décor not missing a detail of perfection. It's fresh, crisp, and clean, and no one is here. No distractions. No noise. Calm. Just me alone with God and all sorts of reflections of his beauty.

I find peace.
Deep breaths.

I've longed for you, missed you. Here you are.

I inhale in the moment, this gift of grace, and I thank God.

Look for Peace

A few short weeks ago, the currents of life were dense. A little thicker than the usual, and my lifelong friend Jessica had invited me to visit her new lake home for a solo writing getaway whenever I could escape for the day. For the record, this tranquil backdrop, which I could never do justice in describing, is not my typical writing environment. You may be skimming my best chapter yet, and if so, I may have to return to this sweet spot more often. But my norm is pounding on the keys of my Chromebook, earbuds of white noise drowning out the background chaos of a house of seven (plus Sandy, our six-year-old Shih Pom) in chopped-up segments of time, sure to squander creative streaks and intense depth of thought.

What a luxury to relocate seventy miles south, away from the real world, into a space where inspiration receives liberty to flow freely, and my capacity increases to tune in to the uninterrupted Holy Spirit for words to pour out in hopes of serving others. I am so thankful. For this time, for God's gifts wrapped in relaxation, for friends with fantastic lake houses (no doubt), and for much-needed peace.

Real quick, if you're longing for, starved for, peace, renewal, and repose, can I encourage you to seek out a carefree accommodation you can visit for a brief fill-up? Boy oh boy, is it beyond worth it.

But I almost didn't make it here. Storms were forecast. Yep, that slithery snake, for sure. He didn't want me here. I can see why now. And he conned me, since I see no storms. It's breathtakingly gorgeous. In fact, I bet it would be if there were storms too. That's what I was banking on. I noticed the 70 percent chance of severe weather about a week before I made the trip. Okay, not ideal, but anything can happen, so I waited it out.

Then two mornings ago, a text popped up, "HAIL!" It was Jessica, and her predictions were spiraling worse. Heavy storms now written up in the weather report, and my confidence stuttered. Satan knows weather is a worry trigger for me. But here's what I knew—that he'd be hot after me and I should be expecting him to throw stones to hold me hostage in my safe place. You know, the place I have to plug up with headphones to drown out the racket and clamor. So, I had armored up. I was called and determined to head to a quiet place (with the victor over all storms, mind you) to find and write about God's peace, and I couldn't let a potential storm, or Satan, stop me. No sir.

We can't ever really hide from storms anyway, can we? Aren't they always in the forecast? Maybe not tomorrow. But sooner or later, they come, they pass. Calm in between. Blue. Still. Storms come again.

Peace in the Storm

And isn't this life?

Storms perpetually on the horizon. One gust of wind away from the next catastrophe or anxiety attack. One cloud away from a dreary, dark day of despair or discouragement. The only difference between life and weather turbulence is that you have no meteorologist or radar app to warn you when the brutal blows are coming. We grasp hard for glimpses of the future. Fortune-tellers, tarot cards, and horoscopes make a bunch of smarty-pants people rich in their efforts to make a dollar off the gullible ones who can't stand not knowing what's coming. But it's all fake, smoke and mirrors. Sorry to disappoint. Truth is, only God knows when and what storms are on our path ahead. And for reasons known by him alone, he wants to keep it that way.

And truly, though we've gotten all techy with our weather-detecting devices, I still couldn't be 100 percent sure what physical storms would greet me at this peaceful haven today. But how ironic I was running from the little life storms at home to retreat to peace, only to anticipate visible storms that might also rock the boat of comfort and contentment.

This is the life of worry at its finest. The residue of anxiety from habitual worry slowly erodes all peace from all places that could be, should be, beautiful and life-giving. Peaceful. Full of peace.

> The residue of anxiety from habitual worry slowly erodes all peace from all places that could be, should be, beautiful and life-giving.

We want peace. But as storms are inevitable and unpredictable, the only way to find it is to learn to look for its calming force through the inconsistent elements. Search in the monotonous drizzle, peer through gusty downpours. Seek peace, regardless of the blast and blare. Peace that overtakes and overrides worry. And sometimes the storm waits, sometimes it breaks, and sometimes you prepare for and expect it, but it doesn't come, and you receive the blessing of an even richer deposit that trickles over into the windy moments ahead.

How did I gather the strength and confidence to plow calmly into what looked like storms, head-on? Was it stored up in the safe of my soul? And when we look, but can't find peace, where do we borrow it from to face the disturbance?

Choosing Peace

Within. Yes, it blossoms from the fuel of our thoughts and minds. Your emotions and reactions gather it from the words etched in your heart. The songs you have been singing to your spirit day in and day out.

We are all famished to unleash peace in our lives. We want to keep peace. Sustaining peace. Our most powerful weapon against worry, I might add. But when the mind is filled with worry, a state of anxiousness smothers the scent and sound of serenity. It's no news to you that overdosing on worry regularly eats up all your stores of peace. But filling up on consistent feedings of peace allows peace to be the fuel we thrive on and fight off worry with.

Here's some good news. Remember we highlighted in Chapter One how we have some say over our choices? Likewise, because we can choose what to eat, what to put into our heads and hearts, we can choose peace. Peace and worry can't coexist. So, by choosing peace, choosing to dwell on God's goodness and grace, we are choosing to fight off fear and worry.

What does that look like in our life? What are your practices of choosing peace? Now that we're moving into relearning, we'll keep adopting healthy habits to replace destructive worry-inducing routines.

> But filling up on consistent feedings of peace allows peace to be the fuel we thrive on and fight off worry with.

Let's consider what we have been choosing to feed on. Have you been pouring healthy nourishment in and out from your soul? The flourishing fruit of God? Well, God's good fruit is available to us and from us. That sustained peace we're hunting down comes only from him. It is a fruit of the Spirit, directly opposite fear and worry. So, if it looks, tastes, sounds, and corresponds with God's biblical peace, soak it in. Practice that. This was me in nature today. I figure if I'm going to practice seeking peace, I need to place myself more regularly in God's worry-free natural creation. A mere five yards from my current comfort.

Peace in God's Creation

I finally made my way down the steep set of stairs to the still water. So glad I did.

The sun will set in a few short hours, but now, its warmth pierces my skin and seeps through. I rest. Eyelids squint, legs on lounger. There's a breeze that grazes me. Varies like waves off the ocean. Light, subtle, then swift, steady. The water sparkles brighter now. Magnified diamonds dancing. Birds soar. What are their names? Where is Mike (my bird-loving husband)? He would know and would love it here. God knows. God is here. This much I'm sure of. In this place. This good place. All his. Good gifts.

I looked for him. God. And found him.

I found peace. God's peace. The peace that feeds. The peace that sustains.

We find peace when we find God. And God's peace in nature is just steps outside your back door. I wonder why I don't run to and notice her dazzle more often. I may be inches away from a picture-perfect, divine earth-water-sky scene at the moment, but every bitty bit of God's creation is swelling with his handiwork.

Open the gift of pristine freshly fallen snow, the majesty of layered billowing storm clouds, booming broad thunder, massive bolts of electric lightning. The kaleidoscope of wildflowers scattered over rolling countryside, the delicate budding of spring blooms, the allure of multicolored autumn leaves, and the symphonic sounds of summer nights.

> We find peace when we find God.

Look for it and you'll see it. Drink it in. Drench yourself in its blessing and beauty and find God's love. A love pouring through all things that casts out fear and launches deep peace.

And could I find such peace if I didn't look for it, didn't look for God, or allowed worry a place here? Not a chance.

God. His creation. Peace. See it. Open it up. Practice it.

Practicing Peace

Now sadly, you won't always be able to find such visible calm in the chaos of your day. Not all moments are totally alone with the Lord. So, most of the time you might need to rely on more practical tangible means. I'm just now learning to spend more time in the natural world, but I've long been developing other tried-and-true peace practices and seeking my own worry-squashing techniques. I've got to pass them on to you. But before I do that, hear this billboard truth: Consistency is the key. The key to fighting back against anxiety, worry, fear, and the storms of life and replacing them permanently with peace. Feed often, regularly, again and again and again on these peace-inducing indulgences and watch stillness settle over your renewed spirit. Did I say "consistency"? Good. Don't forget it. It's key. I said that too. Great. Hopefully it will stick now.

> Consistency is the key. The key to fighting back against anxiety, worry, fear, and the storms of life and replacing them permanently with peace.

Every day. Every morning. Before my device hits the palm of my hand. Well, maybe that part is a bit of a stretch. Working goals, right? But the daily plan is devotions, prayer, journal, Bible study. Regularly. Regardless of where I am and who tries to mess with me. These things await my habitual encounter. And let me just tell you how incredibly they have permeated more peace in the remaining flow of the day.

It's not as simple as consistently checking four boxes, though. There's intentional focus required, hence no phones or people messing with me. It starts with my devotional reading, which is much more than simply reading. If any one of us tries to consume a few paragraphs with half-shut eyelids, sleep clouding the clusters of complex words, complete with cobwebs of an aging brain, you're borderline wasting precious time. I guzzle twenty ounces of water waiting by the master bathroom sink, slip on my slippers, tiptoe to the coffeemaker so as not to wake a soul (okay, most days it's Mike), and return to my bedroom upholstered desk chair to allow the warm aroma to waken my senses as I sit and set my eyes on the Lord.

Devotions and Scripture

I begin my first drowsy read-through of that date's devotion and Scripture—Sarah Young's *Jesus Calling* is my current go-to. After which I sip down another swallow of hot black brew and recite the internal words "Lord, open my heart, and soften my soul." With a long pause, an inhale of heaven's breath surrounding me, and a lowering of shoulders releasing the tension of worldly pressure, I next commence a second reading. Which concludes with corresponding Bible passages. Every. Single. Morning.

I imagine Jesus beside me speaking the words I pore over. One or two words at a time. Slowly. Three more. I ponder. A few more. Absorbing into my life. Another phrase. Focus. Repeat that one. *Lord, what do you want me to hear?* More words gradually soaking in. How can I apply them? Refocus. *Jesus, give me your thoughts and your mind.* Repeat again. Crawling through his melodies. Reflecting, delighting, meditating, conversing with my Maker. Divine reading, I've heard it called. Ingesting words, meditating on how God wants to speak them to me, and drawing in nourishment from his presence and whispers. It certainly feels divine. It's intentional, concentered; it's zeroed in on discerning his personal proclamations intended just for me.

Prayer

And then I close my devotional time in undisturbed prayer. I described my prayer habits in Chapter Four, but for the sake of stressing consistency and priority practices, I'd like to whip through another rundown from a different angle. It's that important to note again for sure. Not to mention, that was a few chapters ago, maybe (but hopefully not) such a while back you've already forgotten. But nonetheless, worth mentioning as I believe prayer should be your number one consistency practice.

Recall the encouragement in 1 Thessalonians to "pray without ceasing." So, here we are again, in devotionals, praying continuously—through our reading. And almost as if the conversation doesn't skip a note, the prayer goes on. I close the book, hands folded, head bowed, pursuing intimate conversation with my loving, listening, ever-present Father. I share. Some off-the-cuff variation of my triple As (awe, ask, admit). How thankful I am for all that he is and does, how much tending-to I need with this and that, and anything else that I need to get off my chest and release.

I spill. I linger. And listen. There is peace in the lingering and listening. I let it last. Long and longer.

And here's what emerges: more peace.

Because when you soak in God's peace, worry dissolves, and as worry dissolves, peace evolves.

> I believe prayer should be your number one consistency practice.

Journal

My daily aspiration to journal follows. Notice I didn't say "my daily ritual." The two above are nonnegotiable, but from here forward, let's just say some seasons are more habitual than others. But especially during challenging periods when I need larger draughts of peace, I reignite the custom. I pick up my pencil and gold-foil embossed soft peach notebook. Lead to paper, I unload. This wasn't my own idea. The dear counselor-turned-friend I vented my struggles to years back gave me this brilliant idea. And what a blessing she was, and it has been. I pen something like *How am I feeling today? How do I feel about that? What would God say about my sentiments? What would I say back?* Unraveling the threads of my thoughts with my Savior who hears and helps. Oh, how this practice refreshes and restores. You really ought to give it a try it if you haven't yet. I fell in love. Peace therapy, it became. And believe it or not, it was this method of practicing peace consistently that fired up my passion to write and encourage others with my struggles and successes. Pretty cool, I thought.

Bible Study

Lastly, and just as important as prayer (also during my on-my-game stretches of life), I incorporate divine Bible reading, purposeful inspection of the God-breathed Word. I've been known to reverse this order and study the Bible before my devotions (which of course always include Scripture). But whether I choose to begin my break of day with his life manual or plunge into post–quiet time with these shields of harmony, both satiate me with his sufficient wisdom and wonder.

In the early stage of following my calling to become a Christian writer, I had the privilege of being ordained into ministry at my church. One of the curriculum plans included Scripture memorization. And I don't mean a famous verse or two. A huge chunk that might be near impossible to memorize without a daily run-through for no less than a half year. (John 15:1–17, if you're curious.) But here's the magic that happened with time—surely all part of the master plan. The memorized words of the Gospel became my food and fuel. They melted into the mold of my heart, becoming songs meshed into the fibers of my being. Glorious!

Read the Bible. Start with a Gospel, Psalms, Proverbs, or Google a Bible plan. Read a chapter, half chapter, or a handful of verses. Underline, reread, memorize. Note your thoughts, jot down your questions, highlight and script your favorite verses. You don't have to go nuts. Bite off only what you can chew, bookmark the verse you stop on, and pick back up tomorrow. God's words are never wasted, and this time will always serve you well.

> The memorized words of the Gospel became my food and fuel. They melted into the mold of my heart, becoming songs meshed into the fibers of my being.

If you're not seasoned with Bible reading, look up a study at your local church or a church nearby. Fill up on fellowship with other believers seeking God's Word with you. Bible studies are God's gift to the hard-to-Bible-discipline folks (been there) needing practical guidance and a support group. Community to hold you accountable and help decipher what is foreign to you. Piggyback one study after another. Make it a habit. Work Bible study homework into your morning ritual or wherever you can fit it into your schedule.

Devotions, prayer, journaling, Bible study, time with the Lord. The point here: Pick your practices, choose them daily, consistently, and make them habits. Make time for them. Create the space and the stillness for them. If you're lacking peace and aren't practicing peace daily, you have nowhere to direct fingers but at the mirror. (I'm preaching to me too, FYI.)

After picking up the memo over and over, I eventually began heeding the advice to set my alarm thirty minutes before my need-to-be-up time. I may have previously encouraged giving God fifteen minutes at daybreak, but I've found I need more. Let's face it, the more worry, the more the boat of life is rocking, the more stillness and silence we need. You'll know you're ready to stroll on into your day when touches of tranquility sweep over you. Thirty is my new bare minimum. But, I'm working on stealing more minutes. Who wouldn't? This stuff works wonders!

And don't think only the morning is for peace-making time. When the day is disrupted and caves to disorder, and peace is scant and scarce, create a mellow moment. Escape to mental solitude. Repeat as needed. Cover your ears and eyes, even if it's only possible for a half second. And retreat to the aloneness of your mind.

But remember not to let one rising of the sun pass without giving your undivided attention to God. I've been known to sabotage my own morning by sleeping through my thirty minutes, but you best believe my devotional, or some godly book, runs out the door with me and isn't allowed to escape my sight all the way to whatever kids' ballgame I'm racing off to, until I've prayed over the message and gleaned what God needs to fuel me with for the marathon ahead. Or, whatever it is that casts you off and away in the morning. Work? Fine. Take it. Let someone see you. Meeting friends? Even better. They need lots of Jesus, and your inspiration too. Just don't leave the house without it. You need the peace. Or you will.

> Remember not to let one rising of the sun pass without giving your undivided attention to God.

The world won't give you peace. Only God can do that (John 14:27). Take him with you into the world. Take a book with you too. You never know when you'll have a waiting moment. Waiting at the doctor's office, in the carpool line, at a ball or play practice, on a lunch break, or for someone to show up for a meeting. Moments to pick up and soak in peace. Take peace with you into the world.

We make room for what matters. We create time for what we want. We practice where we want to see progress. Do you want peace? Do you want to worry less? If you want it, it truly can be yours. Any day. At any moment. In all moments.

I want you to understand, peace is found in the intentional pause, not in the hurry. So, pause. You have to allow, maybe force, yourself to slow down. You have to do this with the Lord. And you have to practice it every day, throughout your day.

Consistency is the key to sustaining peace.

> Peace is found in the intentional pause.
> not in the hurry.

Fruit of the Spirit

But, consistent spiritual practices produce exceptionally more than peace alone. John 15:4–5 says if we remain in him, we will produce fruit. By the way, *Remain = Consistent.* And Galatians 5:22–23 gives us a peek at what that fruit looks like. The fruits of the Spirit. They are love, joy, peace, patience, kindness, goodness, faithfulness, gentleness, and self-control. Tell me you don't long for more of all that. Notice the third one introduced is our friend *peace*, the lovely fruit we are hard after and aching for. The fruit that, when we consistently remain in God, makes a powerful appearance. But we are cultivating far more than peace in our consistent efforts. A harvest that yields even greater harmony of the heart.

Love. When we're immersed in God's Word, enriched with the knowledge of his perfect love for us as his beloved children, we find peace in the love billowing and abounding as we bathe ourselves in its truth and benefits. Soul unity continues to sprout, and we become more able to receive and pour forth the love permeating us as commanded from the instruction we drink in and apply. God's love turns to peace. Peace to love.

> **God's love turns to peace. Peace to love.**

And joy. When we come across and create joy, a tranquil fragrance swells within. I sense it when I pause, catch my breath, and snag a glimpse of joy in my children. Five of God's sweetest gifts. Have you felt this? A smile or laughter of a child that settles an anxious moment with a sweeping shush and lull of thankfulness. Joy blooms and then peace flowers.

Patience. I wildly want more of this virtue. Don't you? Ahhh. There is so much peace wrapped up with a beautiful bow on top of the stunning package of patience. When I am at rest in peace, patience flows smooth and natural. And when I can follow God's command to be patient, peace drips and melts like honey from this delicious, soul-quenching crop. Want peace? Practice patience. Want to be more patient? Practice peace.

Kindness, goodness, gentleness . . . God's heart is brimming with these peace-breeding blessings. When I corral his peace, kindness is close to my lips, goodness flows freely from my heart, and gentleness is second nature to every move of my hands. As kind, good, gentle actions emerge from the godly nurturing of my soul, I prompt more peace.

Faithfulness. We should all crave this fulfilling fruit: to be faithful in our persevering pursuit of God, to be faithful to others. When we are at peace, this trait is much more attainable than when we might be consumed with rash emotions or behaving irrationally, lacking peace. When we seek faithfulness to God and others, an inner peace is spurred, be it from a clean conscience or the blessing of the Holy Spirit for honoring the Lord. In our faithfulness, peace emerges and expands.

> ### In our faithfulness, peace emerges and expands.

And where is *peace* in self-control? Well, imagine the opposite. Where is peace when we are out of control? Just saying those three words robs the peace and calm from the equation. But self-control persuades peace, and peace provokes self-control. I see it in my little ones. And teens. A controlled, peace-filled disciplinary tone makes way for a calm, direct, receptive eye. Then when I lose it, and I'm sure my contorted look scares with distress and disharmony, I rustle up an unruly response sure to wipe out any trace of serenity. On the contrary, my peacefulness opens the gate to self-restraint. And self-composure and control fans the flame of peace. In you and around you.

Infinite fruit is found when we seek and find his peace. Rewards, blessings, bountiful produce launched in you and around you when you remain in him. If it is love you are after, go to him. Joy, seek him. Patience, find him. Kindness, goodness, pull him in. Faithfulness and gentleness, reel him in. Self-control, draw close to him. And closer. Deep peace? Sit with him, and don't let him go. Remain consistently in him.

Practice peace, dear friend. Whatever you do, wherever you go, place your eyes on him. Your heart on him. Set your thoughts, budding with the sweet fruits of the Holy Spirit, your plans focused on his glory, the intentions and essence of your life, firm, anchored, locked in, on him.

> Finally, brothers and sisters, whatever is true, whatever is noble, whatever is right, whatever is pure, whatever is lovely, whatever is admirable—if anything is excellent or praiseworthy—think about such things. Whatever you have learned or received or heard from me, or seen in me—put it into practice. And the God of peace will be with you. (Phil. 4:8–9)

Think of, speak of, and revel in all of God's rich, Spirit-filled, flavorful fruit, and his tender, nourishing peace will be with you.

> Think of, speak of, and revel in all of God's rich, Spirit-filled, flavorful fruit, and his tender, nourishing peace will be with you.

Guard against Worry

Now, you may not necessarily feel an intense yearning for peace, or find yourself smack-dab in the middle of a storm. Perhaps you sense your perceived storms are manageable, or that you have the armor needed to protect you *when* and *if.* Or maybe, to the contrary, you're weathering worry and the wrangle of dreadful turmoil through this very message. Whichever your scenario, storms are unquestionably coming. Storms you aren't expecting. Storms that will blast through your path so fast there won't be time to brace yourself or seek shelter. And so, we need to be preparing, protecting, and guarding every bit of our being right now.

Philippians 4:6–7 tells us not to be anxious or worry, but at all times to go to God giving thanks, presenting our concerns to him (don't miss the "give thanks" part). And when we do this, an absolute peace presents itself. A peace that transcends, that goes beyond all understanding, all our comprehension. And guards our hearts and protects our minds.

The peace you are gathering and establishing with God can do far more than dissolve your current fears. When you also thank him at all times—regardless of the existence of your ideal environment, in and through the rough patches and storms—an even greater peace blossoms and builds. A mature peace that guards your heart from future upheavals and unforeseen events. A peace beyond all understanding, exceeding all our comprehension. And with God, in his Word and through his promises, this is fact.

Peace will guard you. Peace will protect you. When you lift up your life and give him sincere thanks, raising your cares, your fusses and failures to him. All to him. All from him and for him. Offer thanks for what you have. Offer what you have to God. And receive peace. And the divine melting away of worry.

Sustained Peace in Him

Keynote: Sustained peace that breaks down your rooted fear stems from the Lord alone. Essentially everything we are learning and growing through in faith together is releasing worry and promoting sustaining peace. The more we choose to look for and feed on God and his truths consistently, the more worry-free, peace-filled output will break through to our daily lives. That's radiant freedom from fear, my friend! As thoughts turn to actions, which turn into new healthy habits, doors fly wide open to a sea of blessings. And newfound joy manifests and unfolds within and around you. (More to come in Chapter Eight on that exciting news!)

> Sustained peace that breaks down your
> rooted fears stems from the Lord alone.

But, what if the storm had indeed come today? What peace would have filled my soul? In truth, the storm will come. Eventually. I can count on it. But as worry continues waning, peace is beginning to remain steady. And so it will be with you. As you stand solid. On the rock of God's Word and faithfulness. Certain of his perfect love and goodness. With him, because of him, we can always have peace. And then even greater peace as our confidence in his promises matures and grows. Unleashing peace. Winning over worry.

I am home now. Where commotion is frequent and storms are guaranteed. An adolescent arguing with a toddler, a familiar squeal from the other for always unknown reasons, Sandy barking at the delivery man approaching the front porch. I press hands against ears, resisting the tug of war with my mind trying to draw me away from the constant soothing call of the Lord. Ahhhh. An earned stillness lingers. I shut my eyes and tap in to the deposits of tranquility I've placed in the vault of my longing heart. God's gifts, treasures of heaven on earth, seen and unseen.

And again . . .

I find peace.

I find peace because I long for it.

I find peace because I look for it, for him.

I find peace because it is the song written deeply in my soul.

I find peace because I trust in the faithful, almighty, loving Lord.

I pray you will choose to unleash peace too. She is lovely, and she is always there. And he, the loving Lord, is ready and waiting to bless you with her.

Deeply.

REFLECTION QUESTIONS

1. Where are you looking for peace? When and where do you most often find it?

2. What are your consistent peace practices? What works and what can you add?

3. Do you find it hard to find peace in the storms of life? Explain.

4. Describe what your life might look like if you truly trusted God's faithfulness, love, and power through your current worries, fears, and struggles.

EIGHT

UNLEASH YOUR JOY
Overcoming Dread and Discontentment

June 21

"Don't rush into My Presence with time-consciousness gnawing at your mind. I dwell in timelessness: I am, I was, I will always be." —Sarah Young[1]

Convicted.

My closing text last night had confidently stated, "Y'all are making it so tempting to ditch work and come along! Unfortunately, I will have to join next time."

And just like that, I had turned down yet another summer fun activity (boating, a personal favorite) to crunch on a looming deadline. A target date creeping frighteningly closer, and drawing up an unsettled conscience and uneasy decision receptors. Time-consciousness gnawing at my mind.

I wasn't exactly pumped to get to work this morning. (You've been there, I'm sure.) In fact, I've been dragging my feet in the

---

[1]Sarah Young, *Jesus Calling: 365 Devotions with Real-Life Stories* (Nashville: Thomas Nelson, 2019).

thick sand for a week or so with zero zest of inspiration, weighed down by overcrowded tasks and to-dos. But I knew I had to get back to it. Because, you know, the time clock was a-ticking.

I was positive God would provide the fuel and wisdom, as he always does. So, in typical fashion, I cozied up with my hot half-caff coffee, opened my heart and devotions, and those words of Sarah Young's smacked me square in the face, falling firmly into the corners of my heart.

Yes, I was convicted. I had been playing God of my time—like a rock star, I must say. (Even though I have no business there.) Here I was, preparing to hash out winning over worry and unleashing joy, while searching the depths of my discernment for how this relates to my life. *What brings me that hard-to-find commodity "joy"? When have I let worry steal this sweet fruit?* Surely tons of times.

And lo and behold, it was happening to me in real time. I was presented with joy. Yet saying no to joy, to my girls, in an attempt to master my time. Because of gnawing worry of falling short. My soul lit up like bright flashing neon signs. *Wake up, Keri! These ladies bring you joy! And the water? Joy!* And here I was, hijacking my own happiness with ridiculous worry. Not a chance, Satan!

Sara had invited our Bible study for a day cruise along the Ohio River for lunch. Anyone who could free up their schedule would meet mid-morning at a twenty-minutes-from-my-home marina, cruise down the river to a local water-view savory spot, and float back by 3:00 p.m. I think you got the picture on my Herrington Lake getaway that the water lends me peace. But it can also bring out great joy. Peace, by the way, is most certainly a gateway to joy. Boating in the breeze with a view? Peace *and* joy. Those vibrant God-sent ladies? Always pure joy!

So here I go. To soak in some fun, friendship, grins, and glee. Besides, per this morning's reminder, he controls my time. This work I'm hammering away at is for him. He will do with it what he will. In his time.

As for me, I'm off to delight in a beautiful sunshiny day, glistening water, and blessed time with my people. God's sweetest blessings packed with limitless joy.

> Peace, by the way, is most certainly a gateway to joy.

Worry Steals Joy

Six hours later . . .

Well, would you believe it? I was right.

I most certainly did find some joy. This morning, as I followed through with my intentional first-fruit seeking and obedient yes moments, they led me away from the enemy's attempt to sabotage my happy happenings. Oh, my goodness, dare I declare—God's people do bring me such joy! Their stories, their love, their image-bearing unique giftedness arouse a gladness of spirit that I've come to crave. I look, I listen, and find joy! On top of the spot-on crisp, solid blue-sky weather, the beach-bum music adding the perfect touch of charm, my newfound love "Diet Dr. Pepper" keeping cool, thirst-quenching company, and the shrimp tacos at the riverside diner inducing taste-bud bliss. I collected all the delight I had been needing to spark my dreary soul. And I didn't miss it this time.

What brings you joy? Is it people? Your friends from high school or college? A sibling? Your dad or mom? One-on-one time with your kids? Their smiles and laughter? Their jokes or jabs? Their excitement to share new news? Ballgames? Watching your favorite sports team or TV show? Anyone else find joy in Great American Family? Don't hate me. Okay, ESPN, Netflix, anything? Grazing your toes along the shallows of the seashore? Phone calls from your grandkids? Celebrating birthdays, anniversaries, Christmas, New Year's? At the beach? (Me!) How about visiting a new city? Or country? Or going to the same place maybe for the tenth time because it's that good. Or . . . you dream it up!

I love date nights anywhere. And staring at the ocean in the early morning and under the stars. And hazelnut lattes. And all the ladies in both my Bible study and moms' small group. And long chats on the phone with my mom. Watching my kids play and laugh together. Bike rides along highway 30A. A shaded breezy ballpark seat at a Cincinnati Reds game. Catching a genuine smile on Michael's face. Witnessing the exchange of Christian wedding vows. Cheering on a win of one of my favorite three athletes. (The twins haven't received the go-ahead to embark on organized sports yet.) Raising praise hands to my favorite worship song on Sunday. Yes! So much joy. And I could get even more carried away.

But here's the cruel thing about worry in regard to joy. All that stuff I just rattled off that fills me up with great cheer is robbed right out of my reach by stinking worry. By the lies of my control, my anxious what-ifs, and no-good focus on the storms. The fun-sucking bamboozler hard at work. He does it to you too. Ugh!

Point-blank, worry steals joy.

> **Worry steals joy.**

So, what worries snatch away your joy? My little convicted moment this morning was only a blip of an example of how the nasty worries of life can derail joy and cause us to miss out on potential bliss-producing moments. It can look like all sorts of things. What is it for you? Worry about not enough time? What will so-and-so think or say? What if I fail? What if I miss the better thing? Maybe it's sickness or injury, money or relationships? You may need to think back to the slew of worries and the foundational fears you dug up in the first couple of chapters. All that unresolved junk will interfere with your state of contentment. No doubt about it!

I'd say we've established pretty clearly how worry is woven through more aspects of your life than you'd realized or want to admit. Likewise, where there is worry, there is most definitely an unfortunate absence or lack of joy. Just as peace and fear can't coexist, neither can joy and worry. Not two peas in a pod. So, if we have the slightest desire to restore or boost joy in this one life we have to live, I'd say we ought to take super seriously reducing our worry with all the means we've trucked through together up to this point.

Quick recap. We've identified and retraced our root fears, called out the true enemy, amped up our prayer life, released control, armed ourselves with God's armor, and practiced peace. All things essential to overcoming the monsters of worry. And now we get to take a sweet step further into God's blessing of winning over worry by indulging in some marvelous joy. You want to *enjoy* your life, don't you? Of course! So, let's learn to live *out* of worry and *in* joy! It's a must. *In joy* to *enjoy*! Deposit that conviction deep down.

Worry Misses Experiences

Now, let me ask, have you ever *not* done something because of worry? Avoided a party for the sake of social anxiety, not taken the trip to your dream destination due to fear of flying or exploring foreign regions, kept your kids from church camp for concern of not reaching the next level on the swim or baseball team. (Or something like this.) And do you think letting apprehension dictate your decisions is a good method of handling them? I mean, if you keep on listening to your screaming worry, you (or someone you love) may very well miss out on some stunning surprises God has waiting for you. You know, like my treasured fellowship with the gorgeous view and my girls that I almost missed. By the way, after saying yes, on that very same day God miraculously helped me crush a quarter of this chapter (as I'd originally hoped). Our God of timelessness is so awesome like that.

> If you keep on listening to your screaming worry, you (or someone you love) may very well miss out on some stunning surprises God has waiting for you.

This doesn't mean you should be reckless or irrational about your time and choices, but if you are consulting with God on an issue or decision and feeling a tug on your heartstrings to do something, maybe it's time to listen to him. Not your deceiving worry and Satan's constant reasons-why-not to do something. The "God" choice will never fail you, my friend.

It's so true, but I forget with the best of them. The whole flying thing. I haven't ventured to that distress in eight years. Now, mind you, I've been a bit preoccupied with the throes of parenting and financially supporting five kids. But imagining lifting off beyond the comfort of my ten-hour-drive-time-max throws hard nauseating fists at my stomach. (Hang with me, though. I'm not bailing on this book without tackling my agonizing giant. Stay tuned to the end. Yikes!)

Or maybe you said yes; you didn't miss the something. You did it and lived it. But also allowed yourself to be loaded down with tormenting worry, semi-suffering through the whole blasted experience. Ring a bell? Catch this.

Worry Misses the Magic of Moments

I wanted a peek of the magic I knew it would be. The pictures flooded my swelling heart with elation for the happy couple and my dear friend. Jessica was marrying off her first daughter in what was to be the most magnificent marital celebration they'd witnessed, set on their twenty sprawling country acres in Kentucky. The candid images brought still shots to vivid life. The rays of sun streaming beside sincere smiles of the bride and groom. The perfectly paired fall shades of decadent bouquets, cheering and offering toasts, beaming bridesmaids and groomsmen reflecting the joy of their loved one's fresh union. Elaborate place settings, plenty of tea lights, and a packed-with-elation dance floor. Smiles, laughter, love, memories in the making. Joy. I could almost taste it.

I hated to miss it. Our fall break just so happened to overlap the same weekend, when we'd arranged to be 660 miles south on the beach, on a preplanned extended family vacation. But I couldn't wait to pick up the phone and get every flawless detail when we returned. I was certain the fairy tale would be as joyous a tale as the enchantment I unveiled with my mind.

But. That's not quite what went down. There was disappointment on the line. And the source? You guessed it. Worry.

I rhetorically questioned. "So, was it wonderful?" And to my surprise, her response, "Well, kind of crazy actually!" Jessica went on to spill how the bridesmaids feasted on the cocktail-hour charcuterie boards hours before the wedding guests, the intended recipients of the deliciousness, had even arrived. *Stress.* In the hurried perfection-seeking hustle her husband, Jason, hopped in the shower a mere twenty minutes before escorting his daughter down the aisle. *Anxiety.* And then she missed his father-of-the-bride speech and her father-in-law's blessing over the meal, all for the sake of tracking down an attendant's car keys while the valet strung fairy lights to light the path for guests exiting. You know, *worrying* about the important stuff. *Not exactly.* In short, she was more doused in worrisome frazzle than the dazzle of what was to be as beautiful, and God blessed, as giving birth to one of her children.

In fact, childbearing is exactly what she compared the sentiment of the whole thing to six months after the chaos faded into the dreamy perfection captured in the photos. But, I bet I don't need to remind you that you can drive this same crazy train with the birth of your babies too. You know the dance. Getting tangled up in worry about when and how the tiny bundle will make her entry. Safely or hazardously, slowly or aggressively, calmly or clamorously. It's a wonder we ever manage to gush over the adored affair with such stress. So yes, while marrying off a child has the potential to be one of God's greatest gifts to parents, just like the gift of their life's debut, we go and make big messes and steal the sweetness with our resolve to control, determination to avoid mishaps, and worry, worry, worry (like Jessica) about things not being perfect.

Her hindsight remarks reflected, *I should not have been the one managing this blessed event.* And also echoed that, yes, there was unnecessary worry that undoubtedly slighted her of full joy. Really, does the worldly stuff we get all wound up with truly matter as much as we make it? Absolutely not. Satan at it again, stealing our joy.

Moral here: Anticipating what might happen suffocates the enjoyment right out of moments, out of life, and leaves us hanging on to nothing but dread and disappointment. I'm guilty too often. And in some cases, when we don't get a handle on our worry, disappointment can escalate to discouragement, or worse—despair. Guilty here too. Please don't let that be you. Let's learn better now. Sorry you had to be the lesson to us all in enjoying our kids' milestone moments, Jess. Lucky for you you've got three more shots to get it right! Or hire help, right?

> Anticipating what might happen suffocates
> the enjoyment right out of moments, out of life,
> and leaves us hanging on to nothing
> but dread and disappointment.

False Reality

The truth is, when we live all wrapped up in our worry, we stagger. Stuck in the false (yes, almost always false) reality of a worst-case scenario where joy is trampled all over and nearly impossible to come by. Think about it. If you're persistently busy assuming the worst, you'll avoid and miss moments altogether, or pass over the joy in the moment because you're so focused on the dreadful things you're convincing yourself will surface, one worry at a time. This joy, which worry steals, is a big fat waste and positively unjustified.

I'll back that up. Based on a quick Google search, loads of researchers agree that up to 90 percent of all the big and little things we anticipate don't actually happen. It's like we're tossing in the trash all but about 10 percent of our joy. How absurd! And you can imagine how living each day with only a fraction of joy has discontentment written all over it. Right? We want to chow down on delight and deliciousness, yet we're basically dumping free fresh gourmet entrées in the garbage can to rot and never be consumed for the scrumptiousness they possess. The very bliss we're lacking. Wasted! So sad.

I got busted for plundering my own joy the week before my first encounter with the Faces of Christ women's retreat. I was about to be blessed with three full kid-free nights away with my dearest friend, Allison, and thirty other spiritually thirsty women to grow in faith and relationship with the Lord. My soul was starving for such a holy manifestation. Then a winter snowstorm popped up in the forecast. And before the predictions even reached a 60 percent probability, I was imagining my car in no-man's-land Indiana in a ditch, stranded, with me injured, on the side of the road. Crazy, I know. I mean, who can experience a smidge of hope of joy in the face of made-up scenarios like this?

My husband was quick to steer my mindset to lighter, more logical places. "Keri, you do realize you're not only potentially suffering once, but worse, you're opening yourself to multiple sufferings? When in reality, you'd probably never suffer at all." He was disclosing the pesky truth that if nothing went wrong, it didn't snow buckets, and I didn't run off the road (likely and likely), I'm guaranteeing self-induced agony repeatedly in my mind. Ridiculous. And if the unlikely freak occurrence struck and I did have to endure something unpleasant, I could simply labor though the struggle a single time. Instead of over and over and over. Not to mention—*Hello, sister! God will be with you and will be there to see you through.* I know this!

Positive-Outcome Scenario

This message is true of all of us. So, if our worry thoughts are mostly false, wouldn't it make genius sense to choose to assume the best or a better-case scenario and gain the joy back? Yes, genius! Just as we chose peace, we can choose to restore some joy to our thoughts too. We choose, find, and practice peace. And open the door to positive thinking. Positive thinking is joy-filled thinking. Thoughts full of more cheer and warm fuzzies. A trained, chosen mindset imagining a positive-outcome scenario.

> If our worry thoughts are mostly false, wouldn't it make genius sense to choose to assume the best or a better-case scenario and gain the joy back?

If I had chosen God's peace to dispel the illusion of ruination, I could've painted a more likely pleasant picture (which was the actual picture in the end). Of roads cleared for safe travel, leisurely driving alongside one of my dearest friends (wasn't it a life-giving weekend, Allison?), and inhaling the loveliness of what was sure to be in store. Watching hopefully for steadily at hand, rejoice-worthy moments. God's presence never leaving, always there, joy blossoming moments.

Yes, what if we cemented our thoughts of what's ahead with truth? Think back to our trusted truths that we shattered our foundational fibs and fears with. The army of annoying worries rooted in our fear of worthlessness or helplessness. Those joy-stealing lies that we knocked down with the truth of (1) God's perfect love (our unconditional worth), and (2) God's all-powerful, almighty ability (our unlimited help).

We can always create positive-case scenarios where joy is abundant because we know these truths. We know that no matter what happens, good or not-so-good seeming, ultimately God has good plans for us. To prosper us, not to harm us, for a hope, and a future (Jer. 29:11). This is positively good news that we can bask in. This is joy!

Amen! Thank you, Lord.

Joy in the Lord

Our deepest desire for fulfillment of the heart is found in God alone. That is the way he created us. We can find joy in all things when we find God in all things. Instead of allowing Satan's deceptive hand of worry to rob our moments of the goodness God intended and laced in all our moments, he designed the perfection of you and me to be completely fulfilled, first and foremost, by him. Enjoyment in him.

> We can find joy in all things when
> we find God in all things.

So, we've got to find him if we long for true joy. And must fight off all rampant worldly distractions and deterrents that are ready and waiting for our eyes to stray, making us susceptible to their charm and deception. When your focus wanders even for a moment, you're being duped by the enemy. Vulnerable and prey to joy blinders and all of his staged darkness of fear, doubt, and distress.

Stay locked in to God's joy. Fixated on him. Practicing leaning hard on, keeping your eyes glued to, and finding him. But how? How when the forces of the world are working overtime to shadow all traces of gladness in him? Even if I feel a slight settling of my most nagging cares and concerns, the war still rages. How then do I resist the debris of worry-induced dread and discontentment? Despair and depression?

Dissipating worry doesn't always promise to unleash joy. Maybe it lends to more peace, but sometimes we want so much more than peace. Besides, bathing in too much peace can make me kind of sleepy. And this world (my house and people), with all its needy expectations, demands loads more than my eyes-half-shut lackadaisical stride through life. The people God entrusted to me deserve, and I want to give, vibrant smiles and energy. Peace is great. I love peace, but I want the fullness of life offered through sheer enjoyment of God's unlimited blessings. You?

Replace Joy: Stealing Worry with Gratitude

So, where do we find joy when we don't feel so joy-filled? When we've reduced worry and peace surfaces, how do we disperse the remaining remnants of anxiousness to unleash the fruit of joy we're missing? For peace, we looked and practiced, and found it in him alone. Similarly, to uncover joy, we look and find it through the practice of divine gratitude.

Offering gratitude to God is our shield in promoting and protecting joy. If 90 percent of the time we are wrong in assuming our worries will surface, we have so much more to be joyful about. So much more we are blessed with than we realize. Gifts from God hidden in every aspect of our path that we can uncover and choose to be thankful for.

Learning to live in joy by giving thanks has to be a choice rehearsed regularly, consistently, persistently. It keeps our focus on what's good, what we have, versus what we are struggling with or suffering through. I'd like to lend you some of my strategies to grow in gratitude. The following are everyday ways to practice being thankful and cultivate enhanced joy in your life.

> Offering gratitude to God is our shield
> in promoting and protecting joy.

Thankful Thoughts

When you understand it can be as straightforward as calling out thankfulness when your fickle mind goes south, finding joy can be as simple as choosing to trade worrisome thoughts for thanks. This is my go-to method when I'm feeling not so thrilled about a social gathering, feeling spent before date nights, or uneasy with my kids being driven around town by someone who isn't me.

I went to a baseball game with Mike last week. We've had great experiences at Great American Ball Park, and others not as good. The difference, worry. I wanted this one to be good. When I began to care for 2.5 seconds about the ninety-five degree expected temps and heat exhaustion (how embarrassing), I said, *Nope, I am thankful for any time away. We'll make the most of it.* Thankful. *There are some great eateries next to the park, and we can cozy up in a booth and watch our team on the big screens. Either way, it'll be swell!* Thankful. Choose thankful. What woeful thoughts can you replace with thanks?

Thankful Ten

If replacing thoughts here and there doesn't do the trick, and masked worry leads me to more bothersome blahs and blues, I've been known to rattle off a "Thankful Ten." On the spot, make a mental list of ten things you're thankful for. Not one, but a minimum of ten. Working? Great, keep going. Still dragging? Keep going! Mike loves it when I pull this one on him to pick him up! (Insert sarcasm.) Spouses make great accountability partners, though, you know? I catch his eyes straying to the uncontrollable unpleasantries of the world now and again and I say, "Go, give me ten!" He rolls his eyes but obliges. And then the sheepish smiles break through. *Hey, I see that joy!* Yep, it works!

Thirty Days of Thankful

But sometimes mental notes of ten or merely replacing thoughts with thankfulness won't cut it. When my world gets darker and drearier, and worry and fear are more stubborn, I have to take more serious measures.

It was about five years ago when I started "thirty days of thankful." I was mashed in the middle of winter with self-diagnosed seasonal depression. Anyone know what I'm talking about? When January punched me in the face, I refused to feel another one of its brutal blows. On New Year's Day I made a post on social media. I confessed my struggle and committed to thirty days of publicly sharing the specific things I was thankful for. And ta-da, best January yet! Something about waking each morning, seeking, searching, looking hard for all the blessings I had to beam and boast about, created a spring of joy and shrinking of concern, defeat, and discouragement. Huge step forward.

I later lost interest in opening the forever of my innermost business online, and I opted to try a journal format. Free from the judgment of looking-for-gossip-and-controversy onlookers. Free to share with God the intimacy of my secret surrender and my gratitude for his never-ending work in and through me and those in my path.

Gratitude Journal

I began scribbling down whatever came to mind. Jotting down my thankful ten, digging up any thankful thought God would breeze through my longing heart. I practiced journaling sincere-joy-stimulating gratitude.

A couple of years later, I was inspired further and deeper by a truly talented fellow writer, Ann Voskamp. This farmer's wife and mom of then six, now seven, who knows loss and brokenness, struggle and anxious living, worry, pain, and fear. Yet she found joy in expressing thankfulness. A thousand times and then some. She learned to be thankful. In the monotony, in the uneasy, in the bitter hard. In the details, the tiniest details, and in the difficulties. She recorded everything in her book *One Thousand Gifts*.[2] And I get it. Consider a gratitude journal, follow Ann's example, and watch beauty unfold before you as you greet your day with joy exposed.

Where can you find joy? What can you be thankful for in the midst of maddening moments and edgy occasions? What thoughts can you replace? What good can you record to take the focus off the fear? In this practicing of gratitude and thanks, you'll surely restore some refreshment and drink in uncovered joy.

---

[2] Ann Voskamp, *One Thousand Gifts: A Dare to Live Fully Right Where You Are* (Nashville: Thomas Nelson, 2011).

Trust First

But it's so hard. It's ridiculously difficult to be thankful when you're enslaved to worry. When you're facing or watching others bear the unbearable. I'm with you. Watching my sister, Amy, battle her husband's Stage IV cancer with their two young boys. I'm living this. I'm worried, scared, hurting for them. Joy, thankfulness? How? It's painfully hard when you're fighting with dread, wrestling with discontent, and on the verge of depression.

In fact, gratitude and joy in tough times are almost impossible without one ingredient. Trust. Without trust in truths that we can rely on. God's truths. The truth that he does love us more than we can imagine, the truth that he will take care of us, and that he is capable of doing just that.

We have to trust him to allow our eyes to open wide enough to see all the tiny and grand things surrounding us. Hidden sometimes, but intentionally placed in our life by God. And in this sweet spot of trust and gratitude, joy seeps in.

> Gratitude and joy in tough times are almost impossible without one ingredient. Trust.

Worry Disguised

It's the middle of the summer. I am weary and I am struggling to find joy today. Am I worried? I didn't think so. It hasn't been blatant. The only thought I can muster to think is: I am tired. I stealthily sneak out of the kitchen. The kids are all settled with lunch. I might have ten minutes if I'm lucky. I stare at my bedroom wall in a trance. It's moments of escape like this that send me dashing to crack a book and get lost in the encouraging starved-for words of whatever Christian author is currently inspiring my senses and circumstances. But today my mind was too worn down to comprehend such musings. The message of my own battle was too loud to quiet the chaos enough to melt me into the mind of another.

I spontaneously picked up my gratitude journal. Not sure how or why. But God moved my fingers to the drawer and walked them to the soft-bound pages untouched for over a month. I was thirsting for joy, and the Lord prompted those same fingers to pick up a pen and record thankfulness.

What can I possibly say?

Deep thought . . .

I *am* worried. Worry. It stirred up. I didn't want to call it that. And I don't want to admit I haven't focused on God's goodness and ability. Or that I haven't been thankful and have allowed grumbling to slip in.

The enemy wants me blind to my lack of trust and gratitude. He softens it and whispers, "You're just tired, weary. No shame in that." My worry, his lies, are disguised as a tired soul that simply needs some shut-eye, a massage, and a spa day. (A girl can dream.)

But while it's true I need refreshing from beating myself down with joy-deficient anxious striving, a worn-out will to control, and wallowing worry, what I really need is to rest in him.

And yes, in him I find my rest. And I am thankful.

Worry lurks, but in him, I can be thankful.

I remember Jesus, and I am thankful for his relentless love, dying to free us from our chains, stains, and strains. Sunday morning we bow our heads, sip the blood, and partake of the broken body. And fears fade and joy emerges in our remembrance, thankfulness, and trust.

Trust through Worry to Joy

Underneath it all, more than anything, I am thankful for my knowledge of the truth that the Lord loves us and always provides sufficient strength, comfort, help, and power. Despite the worries. The weariness of summer, the longevity of unease, concern, waiting, and inability to control. The cancer, Amy's struggle to cope, her boy's anguish, writing deadlines, falling short as a summer mom, vibrant wife, encouraging friend. I have let exhausting, crippling doubt creep in and smother joy, and I've neglected gratitude and bold faith.

How do I find thankfulness and joy when so much pain persists? *Relentless trust, Keri.* Unshakable trust, friend.

God, I trust you. I do, I do. I am sorry for not living like it. But, I trust you are in control. I trust you know what you are doing. I trust it is for good. And that is good. And so, from the bottom of our hearts, we can say thank you. And unleash smiles and joy in our hearts pouring into brighter days.

I choose to say *thank you* through the hard. For the sweet scent of summer, blackened bare feet, sun-kissed cheeks, chlorine-stiff heads of hair, late nights and early mornings, a full house of neighbor friends, Sunday dinners at Amy's, deep chats and tender hugs with my beloved nephews (Jake and Josh), scattered smudge footprints across the kitchen floor, celebratory walks with Mike at the finish of a chapter. Grandparents grabbing the kids for poolside memories, mellow I-get-it moments with Mike, and country music over impromptu cookouts. Finding thanks in the hard. I trust. I am thankful. I am joyful.

Use Your Worry for Joy

As we become grounded in trust and thankfulness, our abundance cup begins to fill (Rom. 15:13). Joy brims at the surface and becomes a familiar tune. You'll want to share it. And a little joy tip: you should! I've tested it out, and here's what I've found. When we share our joy in service to others in need of joy, in need of God's love, in need of a helping hand, in need of rescue from fear, we find more joy. As a hardwired worrier who now encourages and serves others with her own war with worry, I've learned God has a beautiful way of whipping up an infectious joyful purpose in our hearts when we serve and come alongside his people on his behalf.

We can help ourselves and we can help others. Everyone struggles with worry. Everyone wants more joy. Everyone needs to learn to trust God.

> God has a beautiful way of whipping up an infectious joyful purpose in our hearts when we serve and come alongside his people on his behalf.

Unleash Joy

Friends, if we don't fully, with all that we are, trust God, we might only experience moments of joy when our circumstances are on point and pristine. But life is a roller coaster of dips and twists, flipping us upside down and sideways into darkness. Perfect doesn't happen. Happy doesn't last. And joy can only manifest in a life that's infected with brokenness and disappointment when we learn to trust God. Trust that he is good. Trust that he has it all. Trust, trust, trust, and be thankful for what he does and who he is.

I know you want more joy in your life. I know the worry and fear that lingers hinders that place of happiness and contentment. But you're making progress. You know worry is a waste. You know now that the majority of negative scenarios you come up with are false, and that you can create a positive new image infused with the truth that God is looking out for you. That he has incredible plans for you and your future. That you have loads to be thankful for. That you can trust the good that is to come. I hope you're feeling this. I hope it's brightening your outlook and welling up within.

You always have hope. You always have something to smile about. And you can keep learning to win over worry, unleashing more joy in you and all around you. Praise God!

REFLECTION QUESTIONS

1. What brings you joy? What joys would you enjoy with less worry?

2. What magic have you missed in moments because of worry? Why?

3. Where do you need to practice gratitude when it comes to the areas you are lacking joy? How can you do this?

4. What would it look like to trust God enough to find the joy in tough times and through your fears? Do you know you can trust him?

NINE

UNLEASH YOUR PURPOSE

Finding Significance in Obedience

What if I move and miss this place? This house that welcomed three newborn babies. These neighbors who have become some of our closest friends and know where the key is hidden on the front porch. This metro county where my husband and I grew up and graduated from high school. The familiar sounds and smells and memories.

What if . . .

What if I part ways with my career to stay home with the kids, and wind up feeling worthless? Or quit for a flexible gig with unpredictable pay, and fall short on the bills?

What if I release my maturing children to the wolves of the world and they end up injured or rejected or broken or lost?

What if I get on that airplane and the engine shuts down or blows up?

If I fall in love, and he falls out?

If I show up solo to the party and no one talks to me? Or likes me?

Or I go for it and flop? Or try, but fail? Or find misery?

On the Other Side of Worry

Well, what if I *what if* and *worry* myself so stinkin' much I miss out on God's goodness planned in the here and now? And ever after. Because what if on the other side of *worry*, and all this *what-if* nonsense, there is *purpose*? And what if I told you it's true.

What if I leave the house that I love for something not-so-seemingly perfect, but two years downstream it leads me to an upgraded home? With neighbors whose kids become besties with mine, memorize my garage code, switch the laundry I forgot in the washer before vacation, and even nice-and-tidy fold the toddler PJs left in the dryer? What if I find that I really am a smaller-town girl at heart and the new scents, sounds, and memories become familiar fast? And I love it. What if I find the new, which I never knew is better?

What if I walk away from that comfortable career, but later find greater comfort in a strong sense that my kids have the love they need day in and day out? When they get off the bus, and when they need help with homework. And unearth a mom with time to fill up with what fuels her, and to pour out to the ministry of her family and friends. What if money is tight, but my dependence on the Lord tightens?

What if my kids do explore wide-open spaces and find love, life, and joy? Or mistakes and lessons, pain and perseverance, injury and healing. What if my release opens the door to freedom, fullness, and God's faithfulness? And fun!

What if the plane takes me somewhere I could never drive to, and it's amazing?

If this one is *the one* God wants me to marry?

Or if I make a new connection at the dreaded function that paves the path to new friendships or opportunities? And inspires me to flourish more often in the company of life-giving people? What if the right people do actually like me?

What if I don't fail, or flop, or fall hard? And I fly. And my worries and fears don't prove true, and it all works out in the end. If I learn, and love the new thing, the new way, the new life. What if I stop playing it safe all the time, stop avoiding and delaying the sweetness and abundance in God's plan for me?

What if I find *purpose?*

Aww, yes . . . I want that. Don't we all?

> **What if on the other side of *worry*, and all this *what-if* nonsense, there is *purpose*? And what if I told you it's true.**

What are the *what-ifs* festering in your fearful fantasies? The confessions I recounted have been many of mine. Yep, lived every single word. Of all of that. But it was the latter, the positive scenarios, that became my reality. Where purpose was unlocked and unleashed. Only as I've learned to stop listening to the worrisome *what-ifs* and start listening to God. Blocking the thoughts that try to convince us we're better off not taking the perceived risk. Those enemy whispers of "You're safe here. Stay safe." But what in the world does he know? We swore off listening to that snake anyhow, right?

Yes, God is the only master who has good purpose planned for us. A plan we can count on. A plan so good because his love is so big. So, doesn't it make much more sense to call on him, lean on him, and listen to him for our decisions? God says, "What if I loved all these what-ifs away?" Because he can and he will. Okay, quick comical interjection. If you didn't notice or don't know country music, that's actually Kane Brown's line in his hit "What

Ifs."[1] My husband couldn't help but bring this tune to the surface when I rattled off my *what-if* examples. But it's true of God too. He longs to love and wash our *what-ifs* far, far away.

Choose Obedience, Choose Blessings

God doesn't want us stuck in that awful avoidance trap. Because that's what tends to happen with the *what-if syndrome*. Avoidance. No, he definitely doesn't always ask us to play it safe and avoid every risk we catch a whiff of. God truly aches for us to find our purpose. To trust his love, to follow his calls and commands, and to be obedient to them. Regardless of risk. God wants us to choose audacious obedience over worry-filled avoidance. And that, my warrior friend, is our armor against avoidance and what I call the *what-if syndrome*. Obedience. Our bold steps toward significance, the path to purpose, the byway to his abundant blessings. Blessings of significance, meaning, and rich, rich purpose.

> God wants us to choose audacious obedience over worry-filled avoidance.

You know, I can't recall when my eyes first skimmed this verse, but I can certainly remember how the warning of Deuteronomy 11:26–27 stirred up my urgency to address my tendency to worry. It reads, "See, I am setting before you today a blessing and a curse— the blessing if you obey the commands of the LORD your God that I am giving you today."

But what I heard was, "If you don't do what God says, Missie, you might very well find yourself up a creek with no paddle." Uh-uh. No way, Jose. No curses for me. Blessings? I'll take a bunch of that, but you can keep your creepy-crawly curses. My life has

---

[1] Kane Brown, "What Ifs," RCA Records Nashville, 2017.

enough mess and mayhem. You? If I have to figure out what course God wants me to take to get to the good stuff, to capture the good life, the better life beaming with purpose, I'm all in to figure that out. I choose the blessing. I'll choose obedience.

Will you choose obedience? To make the moves that squash the what-ifs and worries, stop micro-calculating the potential hazards and downfalls, and run relentlessly after the lavish, luscious fruits of your divine future? Will you take steps of reverence toward purpose and say yes to God?

Maybe you want to. You're ready, you're feeling progress in this win over worry, and you are beside yourself excited to run through the door stripped free of *what-ifs* and drenched in bold yeses for the Lord. On fire to let loose a life lit up with all the greatest goodness God can possibly deliver in and through you! You can almost taste it with your hungry heart, feel it in your aching bones, and visualize it in your longing soul. You're so ready for freedom.

Discernment

The Bible says we'll be blessed, and prosper in all we do, if we walk in obedience (Ps. 128:1, 1 Kings 2:3). Smells like the sweet scent of purpose we're craving. But how? How do we discern what God really wants? How do we find it and know? How can we release the chains of avoidance and walk in obedience if we are clueless regarding what his will is?

These are great questions. I'm so glad you're asking. I'm so glad I asked in my midlife search for significance. And I'm even more glad that I found answers. Because guess what? God absolutely has them for you. I needed to know. I needed to know that I was following God's better-than-mine path and plan. In knowing I was walking his walk for me, I became more worry-free. Free from all those what-ifs. Free from fear of failure and future misfortune. When we are confident in God's way, because we know it is the best way, fear shrinks, allowing peace and joy to bud, and purpose to blossom.

> In knowing I was walking his walk for
> me, I became more worry-free.

So, don't you suppose if we are working on winning over our worry, and can help fight it with assurance in walking in God's purpose, that we should consider doing what it takes to find his answers? I hope you're nodding your head, because I'm with you. And here's how we do this. Discernment. Which we receive by seeking. Seeking his words and seeking his presence.

In my adamant search I dug deep for discernment. I turned to God's Word, and I found God. I found answers, I found freedom from worry. And I found purpose.

Now, you may not personally be well versed on how to find his commands or discern them. I mean, sure, the Bible. But there's like eight-hundred-something thousands of words in that book of instructions. Which ones apply to you at this very moment? And how exactly? Talk about overwhelm. Good thing God makes it super simple for starters with two primary commands. Great place to start. I'll rephrase, *best* place to start. Right here. Number one, *love God*. And a close second, *love others*.

Loving God Leads to Purpose

We love God by seeking him. By growing in intimacy with him, getting to know him, and learning about him and his perfect character. God wants nothing more than to spend time with you. When you seek his presence, you are speaking his primary love language. He's wildly giddy over it. And it's in reveling in his glory and mighty presence, and immersing our being in his luxurious love, that we encounter his nudges and whispers and callings.

I was a half decade into my thirties when I set out on a pursuit of purpose. Uneasy and unsettled is how I would describe my demeanor at the time. What once felt right started to feel a bit wrong. What once worked didn't all of a sudden. For years I had loved the work I was involved in. Was sure God had sent me there. And he had. For a season.

I had grown in my gifts and flourished in my faith. Basked in purpose and pride in my God-given talents, all starting the day I left corporate America to go against culture's grain of the so-called secure nine-to-five. A home-based network marketing business was working for me. Until it didn't. Not because I didn't want it to, but because after some time, apparently God didn't want it to. Anymore. Remember, he is in control, not us.

But I was devoted to making it work and wouldn't let up on one human move if I had anything to do with it. I force-moved my body, and so God force-pushed back within my heart. The passion and ambition I thought would never wither or wane began to do just that as I lost every last spark I tried to fan into a blaze with my will to work harder.

> And it's in reveling in his glory and mighty presence, and immersing our being in his luxurious love, that we encounter his nudges and whispers and callings.

Our Path Unfolds Our Purpose

Though before the last flicker faded, God planted a girl in my business and life. Lori, a sweet new-to-town Louisiana native I met in Bible study, who became a fast friend. She was also in her midthirties and had three kids just like I did, all about the same ages. Our biggest difference, she revealed she hoped for a fourth. Good for her! No way could I handle more kids. I felt past my prime and tapped out in that department. I was searching hard for how God might use me on the work front (that was the new purpose I knew). But more babies? No thank you, sir! That ship has sailed. Or had it? Nudge number one.

My business was sinking and my desire for it had already sunk. And sadly, my purpose felt in jeopardy with them. I had so much to offer. I had seen it. Mike and I had just delivered our "Most Inspirational Leader of the Year" award speech and announced to thousands we aren't stopping. But not stopping *what* is the question that remained. I wanted purpose. For God to use me. And I started to wonder if it was in a new way.

That's when the unease and unsettledness started stalking.

Have you been there? In a season of fulfillment that started fading? Your heart started changing, doors were closing, and your path and future felt shaky and shaded?

It didn't help that I had been studying the book of Revelation in my Bible Study Fellowship (BSF) class. Word to the wise: If you aren't a seasoned student of the Bible and are worry prone (I was a wreck then), maybe don't start with the book of Revelation. Dragons with a bunch of heads, fire and hell, and torturous dark stuff. And it's all for real? Or something like it. Yikes! Anyway, my anxiety was escalating, and I was elated when the study came to a close.

But I was stewing on *What now, God?* and stirring for answers. I longed to steady a sense of purpose. And it was dwindling.

So, I did what most conflicted individuals do next. Blabbed to my best friend about it. Sort of like an explosion of blindfolded sporadic random-fire emotions is more like it. I prefaced the vocal outburst with my confession of amplified anxiety about where I am, what I might do to fix it, and all the options and angles to take to determine *if* and *what* shift God wanted me to take. And at some point, in my rambling of possibilities, these words made their first appearance, "Or maybe I should have another baby." "You're not serious?!" I think she replied.

Maybe I am. Nudge number two.

What had gotten into me? I couldn't possibly be serious. Mike would freak! I'll never forget his semi-joking jab, years back, indicating if we ever had more kids, we'd wind up divorced. Also known as, plate is full. I'm good. Done. And I was 99.9 percent on board with him. That was the almost maxed-out quantified load of my anxiety with the demands of three kids plus my current emotional and mental capacity. I had maybe a measly 0.1 percent left. That wasn't enough for another baby. And even if it were, I didn't want to end up divorced. I love my husband. We've got the greatest gift of a thing going. I said, "I do" and "till death do us part." End of story, folks. So, baby? No, I couldn't be serious. I just seriously needed some hard-core direction from God. Always true.

> I just seriously needed some hard-core direction from God. Always true.

Seeking God, Seeking Purpose

I totally should've started with a closer lean into the Lord at my first sense of unease. And hey, maybe you'll learn from my oversight. But nonetheless, I ramped up the search, and I amped up my time with the only one who could steer me clear to a purpose-filled path. This marked my morning quiet time taking a deliberate deeper dive. I became super dedicated. First thing, plus touch-base points throughout the day. I wanted to hear from God. I wanted to encounter God. So, I sat with him, talked to him, and soaked in his Word, without fail. Each and every morning.

I committed to him. And he spoke. Louder in time. And I began to hear.

I committed to Bible study. I'd skipped the last session and up to this point was never really great at the homework part. I figured, *Hey I'm here. Better than nothing.* And I guess it was. But I wanted more. I wanted to hear from God more. And if you want to hear from God more, you need to give him more. More of your time, your attention, and your heart. I dropped the excuse *I have too much work I need to do and people who need me,* and replaced it with *I have work and people who need me to be the best me God created, and I can't afford not to show up for this, for him.* So, I showed up, did the homework. And God showed up more.

> And if you want to hear from God more,
> you need to give him more.

Of all things, my regular Bible study group had just chosen a book about the mission of motherhood. I remember an early key principle breaking down how our mission in raising children of God is to multiply, not just people, but the Christian community. Also, how we gain great purpose in this as moms. So, as the study unfolded, my conviction and passion of purpose as a mother expanded and evolved. With my three children, and maybe more? To top off the irony, my dear friend Jamie—our current study leader, and yet another midthirties so-called past-her-prime gal—became preggers with a big gap in years since the birth of her previous (would be my story). And somehow, this whole setup became nudge number three.

What was God up to?

I kept on.

I continued my commitment to seek God for guidance like never before. And the nudges and whispers continued rolling in. Faster. And closer. A sermon here and a bunch more there. A divine appointment with an older mom of many, and then another, and another. And books with more and more stories poking and prodding my wonder, *Could it be? Is God telling me to have another child?*

Oh no, maybe so.

Loving Others Leads to Purpose

It beats me where in my purpose-seeking I read about shifting my focus to serving others, or what specific sign directed me to it. But I know that next to "love God," the Word commands us to "love others." So then, doesn't it only make sense when we're seeking God's will and aren't yet 100 percent sure what to do, to make a point to love on people? I thought so. When you feel as though you've invested more richly in loving him, getting to know him, spending more time with him, the next step in obedience—stepping away from worry and into God's purpose, plans, and blessings—ought to include loving others. Serving on God's behalf. You better believe there are oodles and bundles of purpose wrapped up in our outreach.

> You better believe there are oodles and bundles of purpose wrapped up in our outreach.

When Jamie's angel of a baby finally arrived, life dealt her a series of critical circumstances. Her dad's end-stage cancer, the passing of a close family member, and her own mysterious health complications. She was a treasure of a friend. I wanted to help. I wanted to shine God's love on her. And I could see that she needed it. So, I offered to watch little Matthew to allow her to tend to anything she needed to. Self-care, house care, caretaking, whatever could catch her a breath. Mind you, I hadn't held a baby in years. Not since Kaitlyn, my number three, who was five at the time, but is now going on twelve. And friends, I had zero desire for infant snuggles. As I said, that ship had sailed, and I didn't care for it to return. I was *pretty* sure. But God used my service to meld and melt my heart. Hearts fill like that, and sweep up a powdering of purpose, in our service. The good Lord knew what he was doing. He always does.

And this was the straw that broke the camel's back. A nudge that felt more like a stern pull that day. I had to speak up. I couldn't keep these promptings secret anymore. But when was the right time to tell Mike? Never, probably, so I bluntly interrupted our date night thirty minutes in with a news break. I spilled something like, "I've had these thoughts, wonderings, nudges from God . . . maybe."

What he heard. A loud blasting terrifying alarm screaming, "I want a baby!" With echoes of "Your wife has lost her mind." It was not pretty. There was shock and silence, hurt and tears (me). And my defense, "I'm not saying I want a baby . . . necessarily. I just feel like God might be leading us to consider it."

The next few months were full of his *what-ifs* and *are-you-sure's* and repeats of "Again, God's telling you to do what?!" I know, I know. It came as that big a surprise to me too. And I really was still wrestling with the nudge. My heart would have to do some major convincing of my mind. And of course, there was my other half to bring up to speed too.

Keep Seeking, Keep Unraveling

But one thing I was learning. That I kept on doing. Was *seeking*. Do you see what was happening here? In my confusion and quest, I was leaning on God more and more, and he was slowly unraveling my moments, my day-to-day moments, to reveal purpose in the present, and also in days to come. I was learning. Anytime God's callings confuse you, call on him harder. I was getting it. If this was truly God's will for me, for both of us, he would surely speak truth to our hearts. I got even closer. Prayed more, prayed for Mike, prayed for guidance.

And in true God fashion, he plopped the next perfectly fitting Bible study for my situation directly in my lap. Also, my first introduction to my new favorite author. How I missed her up to that point is beyond me, but she was an absolute gift. I bought the coinciding book to maximize the study, and her words and stories and teachings, a godsend. Lysa TerKeurst's *The Best Yes*[2] solidified my yes.

One chapter at a time, Lysa connected with me, related to me, revealed to me the open spaces in my life for God's will and plan, and helped me see clearly, with the Lord as my guide, that I was definitely hearing what I thought I heard. As we seek God more, God speaks more, and louder. *Okay, God, I'm in. I hear you. I don't need any more signs. But you're going to have to work on Mike because I'm not moving forward with something he isn't on board with, with at least half a sincere smile.*

> ### As we seek God more, God speaks more, and louder.

As for me, my cooperative yes was transitioning to a burning *pleeeease God.* I began to want this baby bad. I'd picture family photos with a fourth child. I imagined the kids learning the gift of changing diapers, being Santa Claus, reading him or her books. And heard the roaring laughter that might fill our home. I replaced the *what if we are exhausted, run out of money, can't retire until we're 80, end up raising a lonely only child with the seven-year gap that would be,* with hope. And obedient, purpose-filled what-ifs. *What if I walk in obedience and God blesses each and every person in our house, parents, siblings, grandparents, the whole world, with*

---

[2] Lysa TerKeurst, *The Best Yes: Making Wise Decisions in the Midst of Endless Demands* (Nashville: Thomas Nelson, 2014).

another child of God? Yes, what if all things he calls us to, he uses in the most beautiful ways we never imagined? I studied this truth in a verse in my studies. I clung to it. I knew he had so much more in store than even what I felt called to (Eph. 3:20). So much more.

I finally got that half smile from my husband, and it did become sincere. Praise God.

But then there was the whole I'm-almost-thirty-eight thing. Who knew if I could even bear more children. With the exception of my first pregnancy ending in early miscarriage, I'd been able to conceive three more times within a couple of months. I know, I've been blessed. But that wasn't the story this time. Six months felt like six daunting decades.

I was so sure of what I had heard. In fact, had never been more positive of God's calls on my life in my entire existence. And my slow-to-come-around husband was even beginning to dream about the new family dynamic. Yet, month after month of more than diligent efforts, with no extra pink line.

Faithfulness

What if we do hear God wrong after all? How can we be sure we can trust his direction and nudges? Let me tell you some great news I discovered about the answer to these questions.

It doesn't matter.

What I mean is, you can't go wrong. If you're hard locked in on God, tuned in, seeking him, loving him. You're probably hearing spot-on. And even if you don't, it will *still* work out for good (Rom. 8:28).

Yeah, I know I already recited this verse a few chapters back (for those paying attention), and if you've been a Christian for more than two months, you're surely familiar with it. Or you may even believe this scripture to be overused. But there's good reason. It's got to be a pillar of the faith if there ever were one. Its truth is so rich and glorious. And all the reason you don't have to fear your choices and outcomes. The *why* behind your confidence to walk steady and secure in worry-free obedience. Love God? Great! All things will work out for good! Yes. You heard that right. All. Things.

One more time.

> And we know that in all things God works for the good
> of those who love him, who have been called according
> to his purpose. (Rom. 8:28)

And there's that "purpose" word. We have been called in obedience according to his *purpose*. God has a purpose for you as a Christian, and he will work out your life in order to ensure that purpose, which is actually his. It's all for him, because of him, in him, and through him.

Obedience will not always look or feel super safe, but your *what-if syndrome* can most certainly be replaced and infused with trust in him. Because God is faithful. Always. He promises this. And we have evidence to prove it. In your life, in mine, in Jesus, and in the people of his time.

> God has a purpose for you as a Christian, and
> he will work out your life in order to ensure
> that purpose, which is actually his.

Consider your life. Think back ten years. Is there something you prayed for, something you struggled with, a decision you weren't sure how to make, or a relationship that was rocky? Any of which are now smoothed over, look better, have resolved themselves, or just plain don't matter anymore? Okay, some things might still be in the works, but the majority of the nuances and nuisances of yesteryear that you lifted up to God have made strong shifts in a more pleasant direction. Some sweeter than you ever dreamed. True?

Delight in Him

As for me, I had nothing to fear. I was seeking, persevering, growing closer to God, delighting in him. Walking in faith. The next Lysa book I chose was *What Happens When Women Walk in Faith*.[3] I knew I needed to keep walking faithfully, I knew Lysa's Spirit-guided words had helped me this far, and the flip-flops on the old cover were just my style. She spoke straight to me about the desires of my heart. About God giving us our desires when we delight in him. And I learned I had misunderstood that verse.

> Take delight in the LORD, and he will give you the
> desires of your heart. (Ps. 37:4)

Sure, I delighted in God. And the desire of my heart was now a baby. So, he would grant me that, right? Well, maybe. He most certainly will bless us with our heart's deep yearnings. But here's what's supernaturally awesome. We don't have to worry about getting what we want. When we stay close to him, he has the power to *change* the wildest wishes of our hearts. Just like I didn't originally have a desire for a baby at all. Delight in him . . . *bam*, changed heart's desire!

> When we stay close to him, he has the power
> to *change* the wildest wishes of our hearts.

All I needed to focus on, all you need to hunker down on to fill the emptiness of your heart, is delighting in him. Spend as much time in his Word, in his presence, and tuning in to him as

---

[3]Lysa TerKeurst, *What Happens When Women Walk in Faith: Trusting God Takes You to Amazing Places* (Eugene, OR: Harvest House, 2005).

you can, and rest assured that he will either bring about what you are praying for in time or shift the desires, dreams, and demands nestled in the corners of your heart.

This truth allowed me the sweet privilege of true delight. In him, and in my present purpose. I was reminded that he is in control. Not me. I was reminded that what's more important to him is my heart-sold-out commitment to loving him. Fearlessly trusting in his way and his plan. And resting in that. Not in my grabbing the bull by the horns, or in my desperate ripping away his reins of control. Remember what you wrote in Chapter Five, Keri? There isn't anything you can do to stop God's plan, and there's nothing you can do to prevent it. This baby may not come via immaculate conception, but maybe God has something in mind that looks just a little different than I dreamed. Maybe what we think God is calling us to isn't as black and white as we think. It's his will, and also his way.

I surrendered.

And just like that, over a date night I'll never forget, God opened the heart of the man with dead-bolted chambers in prior months. "If we have to consider adoption," he said, "maybe God has something a little different in mind than we thought." Full surrender. Okay, and some awe-filled tears too.

Loving God, seeking him, delighting in him, surrendering to him. Loving others, serving each other, even serving the unborn and fatherless.

Surrender. To his will, his way.

And the next morning . . . the extra pink line.

Breathless . . .

I can't possibly express in words—it would need its own chapter at the very least—the gamut of heavenly emotions that swirled and danced that morning. I've never experienced more awe of God than I did, face down in the carpet, over collapsed knees, in my master closet at 7:30 a.m. I've never ugly-happy-cried like that in my life either. And I have never felt that extent of overwhelm of Ephesians 3:20.

> Now to him who is able to do immeasurably more than all we ask or imagine, according to his power that is at work within us.

That is, until about six weeks later . . .

I had developed a fear of ultrasounds after my miscarriage trauma at eight weeks with pregnancy number one, so I reminded the tech to quickly state, *Here's the heartbeat*, as soon as she caught sight of the minuscule lifeline. And that she did. Bold as ever, "I have a special surprise for you . . ."

Interesting way to respond to my request, but okay, I thought.

"Here's Baby A's heartbeat . . ."

Fast furious subconscious thoughts flying in a nanosecond. *Wait, "A" means there's a . . . .*

"And here is baby B's."

Unbelievable . . .

Awe . . .

Twins.

Pause. Literal tears just flooded back as I typed those words. You have no idea, or maybe you do, the burst of joy and marvel, and dazzle and wonderment of our big, huge God in such a moment as that, who says "immeasurably more," my love.

So much more.

God had a breathtaking plan. He wanted to share it with me. I sought him, I heard, I washed away the what-ifs and worries and walked boldly. He melted my fears as I clung to him, he worked on my heart, he taught me and tweaked me, and he reminded me of his faithfulness.

He is always faithful.

To me and to you.

Purpose Unleashed

Friends, God has so much in store for you too. Immeasurably more. On the other side of your what-ifs and worries and fears. He has a message for you. A good plan for you. He wants to share it with you. He wants you to get close enough to hear it. And then closer. To free you from worry, to unleash peace, and joy, and brilliant purpose in this very phase, on this very day of your life. Delight in him.

I've made it my mission. Now, I may mess up a lot, as the enemy knows I'm devoted to his archnemesis, and it makes him insanely mad. So, it hasn't been, and certainly won't always be, all rainbows and cupcakes. But the twins have been the sweetest purpose-filled gift to me, Mike, our kids, and our whole extended family in ways we couldn't possibly have dreamed. And I knew God had then, and still has, even more purpose to reveal. He's never done with any one of his children. That includes you.

And so, the pursuit must go on. And it did.

> God has so much in store for you too. Immeasurably more. On the other side of your what-ifs and worries and fears.

I had a blip of postpartum depression ten months after the girls were born. No friend or medication could shake it. But God had more plans to work out with me. In fact, it became the reason I'm writing these words. And I believe he has purpose in these words. In all things he orchestrates.

I pressed on fearlessly seeking, and a Christian therapist encouraged me to journal my thoughts. I began to pray more intentionally and record encouraging notes of truth to myself that

I was certain God would surely speak, casting light into my new struggles. And through my steadfast search, he began to unravel yet another potential plan. A fresh path paving the way to brand-new possibilities and purpose. As a writer. I could love God, and love others, with the encouragement I was receiving. And here I sit now, writing these words to you.

See how God unfolds purpose when we cling to him? Now I have these babies (who are going to be five when these words are published), a faith-filled book in your hands, and have given my life to full-time ministry. Bold relentless seeking, to billowing, blossoming purpose.

Listen, I don't say all this to draw attention my way. You need to know there was a lot of yuck in the middle. The depression was dark. And the road from there to here took years. It's only in the looking back that I can clearly see God's hand. It was foggy in the process at times. But I never let go. I held tight to his promises and his faithfulness.

What I hope and pray for you is that you can catch a glimpse of what it looks like to seek God, struggle with *what if*, seek God, worry some more, seek God, see the light, seek him harder, and learn that in the seeking and walking in obedience toward the whispers, nudges, and tugs on your heartstrings, you will unleash all kinds of purpose in your life. A fullness and completeness and significance like never before.

What is purpose? An ultimate feeling of fulfillment? A brief burst of contentment, a gentle, slow swell of *enough*? A sense of significance in his kingdom? An assurance of God's plan precisely where he has you? All the things that piece-by-itsy-bitsy-piece brought you to your pinpoint of a location? Yes. It's one of these things. It's all of them. It's knowing God is the God of your life. Every detail. He is good and it is good. He brought you to be, and he brought you here. On purpose for a purpose. His purpose.

> In the seeking and walking in obedience toward the whispers, nudges, and tugs on your heartstrings, you will unleash all kinds of purpose in your life.

You most definitely don't have to add a member to your family, craft words from your soul to inspire the world, or work thirty hours a week for a church to find purpose. You can just as easily find and follow sparks of significance behind a desk in a cubicle, meeting a friend for coffee, making a meal for a new neighbor, or counseling your kid through a disappointment. The key to unlearning worry and revealing rich meaning is seeking the good sovereign Lord, discerning his callings, and trusting his perfect love. That will wash away your what-ifs and continue cracking open doors. It's confidently, faithfully walking in obedience, unleashing the blessings of purpose, one season, one day, one moment at a time. In the monotonous or the mundane, in the big and the bold. In the present.

What if on the other side of worry, where you are free to follow in obedience, there is purpose?

What if I told you it's true?

Because it is.

Keep walking with him, and keep winning.

REFLECTION QUESTIONS

1. What are the worries and what-ifs that have led you to avoidance of purpose?

2. Describe a time you chose obedience over the what-ifs, and it turned to blessing. How did you see purpose and significance unfold?

3. Do you find it difficult to discern where God is calling you? What might your worry look like if you leaned closer into God and were confident you were following his path?

4. Are you seeking God's will with *him* to find purpose, or are you chasing *your* way with your will? Do you think you could do better? That there's more in store? Explain.

TEN

UNLEASH YOUR IDENTITY
Taking Flight into Fullness of Life

Numbness, nausea, and nervous belly backflips. My heart is racing. Or has it stopped?

Breathless.

Breathe. God is here.

The wheels spin fast. Faster. I can feel their thundering vibration beneath me. Faster.

My pencil is forcing these thoughts to paper. My hand no longer steady. The words barely legible.

Liftoff.

God is here.

Why still the fear? I struggle to even name it that. I don't want it. I can hardly fight it off. I want to cry. I want faith. Bigger faith. Lord, I choose faith over fear. *Breathe.*

We are in the clouds now. Briefly. Now above. Beautiful. I feel the tears sting and begin to suffocate my sight. I see you . . .

God is here.

Breathe.

My ears catch the muffled sound of the captain. "There are pockets of wind ahead."

Keri, breathe.

God is still here.

And so is the nausea. I swallow hard. Mike reaches over and lays his hand tenderly on my leg. He smiles. "You're flying. You're doing great." I see the loving calm in his eyes. I see his peace. He actually referred to this ginormous floating 737 as a "relaxation pod" as my trembling feet stepped aboard. Really?

How can it be?

God, please wash over me. *Please.* Just a pinch of peace would suffice.

Facing Fear

I have a feeling you know some of these feelings. Maybe it isn't every flight you embark on, but you know, all too well, anxiety, worry, and the fraying of fear on your nervous system. The nause-ating pit of unease. The consuming twist of anxiousness in the gut.

You've made some progress. You've walked steadily with me through digging up the dirt of the past, uprooting the fears hidden at the foundation, praying, surrendering, unleashing God's mighty armor, peace, purpose, and joy. Though we've unlearned some bad habits and entertained some new, there is more work to do. The enemy won't back down. Ever. And we can't stop fighting. Ever.

What we have gathered and gained with the help of the Lord is a lifestyle change. It's putting on faith filters day in and day out, practicing spiritual disciplines and habits. All the armor we've investigated in the past nine chapters.

Sometimes worry will come on stronger, fear will blindside you, when you think you've conquered it, or almost. And the mon-ster of evil will rise to the fight. I feel it in flight. And then you have to battle even harder than you think you're equipped for. There will be these moments and circumstances that trigger a whole new level of fear, or an old familiar feeling of fear you thought you'd buried.

Fear Triggers

Flying is a trigger for me. Obviously, right?

What are your triggers? It will be important to recognize and know them as you continue winning over your worry. What are the situations, experiences, the people, that stir up fear and unsettling thoughts?

Maybe it is flying. Whether of the plane going down, or the loony logistics involved in getting from here to there. Or how about ground travel? I'm about as tense at times on the interstate in a rainstorm as I am sailing above the clouds through the clear blue sky. Maybe public speaking brings out the worry tendencies in you. The heart racing, sweaty palms that show up before you're handed the mic or even prompted to public prayer. What about social gatherings? Small or large, do you find yourself fumbling for words in a crowd, wanting to hide in the bathroom, or riddled with paranoia that someone is questioning your outfit selection, might corner you and bore you, or that no one will want to talk to you at all?

Possibly a person is your trigger. A certain acquaintance or family member who frazzles you. A perceived threat whose looks, responses, lash-outs, or judgment you fear. And so, their presence leaves you on edge, irritable, and uptight. All the unpeaceful things you don't want to be.

Sometimes even movies and the media provoke unrest in your soul. If you expose yourself enough, I can't imagine they wouldn't.

The world is riddled with fuel for our worry. But being aware of our triggers will fire up our fight. I've rehashed many of mine, and I'm sure you can come up with more stimulators that stir the pot of fear in you. Moments past that arise again and again, indicators to disarm your worrier mindset and throw on an extra thick layer of God-trusting-warrior armor. Your true identity that you've been slowly unleashing and unraveling as you've unlearned old no-good habits of control, anxious living, avoidance, and wasteful worry, and adopted a new life of God's strength, peace, purpose, and joy. Your identity in God. Your true self.

> The world is riddled with fuel for our worry. But being aware of our triggers will fire up our fight.

Child of the King

Twenty minutes into the flight now. *"Great is thy faithfulness, O God my Father . . ."* rings loudly in my ears in an attempt to drown out the peace-disrupting ebb and flow of the engine.

Yes, *my Father . . .*

And I, his daughter.

God is here.

Stay focused on him, Keri.

The clouds below me, heavens above, bright blue.

The artistry of his clouds, white mountains. Peaks and valleys of abundant beauty, all under his sovereign control. All his creation. The higher I rise, the closer I feel to my heavenly Father.

Me. Daughter of the Sovereign King. Beloved. Protected.

And I am so thankful.

Only two days ago, I was seated in the third row of the sanctuary on Sunday morning when God reminded me who I am and whose I am. Up until that very day, I had been doing one heck of a great job preparing to face this forever fear of mine. To let you in a little closer, I had decided a few years back that I couldn't rightfully release a book to the world about worry while I was wimping out on tackling my own whopping worries.

> **God reminded me who I am and whose I am.**

Called to Fear

It was the spring of 2020. Everything had shut down, and that included the kids' schools. Seven meandering souls rummaged through cramped lives in the house day after day after day. I was following my call, but wondering where God would take this new path he was guiding me down. I hopped in the minivan and drove about three miles from home to a pond nearby. I parked, picked up my pen and journal, closed my eyes, and asked God to speak to me. A word, a sign, anything. I wanted to know what to do in this very strange, cluttered, chaotic season. That uncertain, unsettled, unsteady season. Just when I opened my eyes, two birds flew in sync over the water, slicing the blue sky in two.

Fly, I heard.

And then there, a jet stream. Almost a cross-shape with the path of the birds.

A plane? Really, God?

Yes. I was sure.

And, as sure as I was of that, I knew, when it was time for this message to take flight, I couldn't show up for you without standing tall with the Lord, against one of my greatest fears.

So, I intentionally chose a nondirect flight (I'm a glutton for punishment, I guess), and Mike and I booked a cute studio ocean-view room at our favorite beach town in all of America. (Of those yet visited anyway. Now that I'm a flight conqueror, I'll keep you posted on our next best find.)

As I was saying, I was checking off each day of the calendar as the day approached with no fear whatsoever. I would think about flying, about our two-day rendezvous, and no worry. *Could I possibly be unlearning this dreading worry?* I started to get so excited at the mere thought. *Has all this emphasis on surrender, prayer, peace, thankfulness and trust eroded my fears and a new me has emerged? Oh Lord, I hope so. This feels so much better.*

And I suppose something new was emerging. In the past, I wouldn't have even had such pleasant thoughts leading up to a trigger event.

But then Sunday morning showed up, and what had been working seemed to stop. Up until then, I had successfully been choosing to replace any semi-fear-resembling-snippet-of-a-thought with positive, thankful foresights. Thoughts of beach moments with Mike, leisurely strolls down Barrett Avenue (a sloping cobblestone street mimicking a picturesque European town), breakfast, lunch, and dinner dates with uninterrupted gazes. Thoughts that swiped out anything anxious with all my peace-filled favorites ahead. And it worked. Until it didn't.

Feel the Fear

As the time was growing closer, and now only two days out, continually suppressing the yuck got harder. The underlying unresolved worry quickly swelled to the point that it seemed as if ignoring the fearful feeling alone was causing added turmoil and unrest in my soul.

It's time to *feel*, I decided.

In fact, sometimes we need to feel the *pain*. We need to feel the reality of the struggle. Because that's where God can help. Where he shows up. Where we get to see his mighty face shine. If your cares are small, uncalled for, unnecessary, or based on your continual focus on the *what-ifs* and negatives, simply switching to positive thoughts and replacing them can be helpful in gaining God's promising perspective. But. If your pain runs deep and the struggles are weighty, a time will come when the fear needs to surface. When you need to feel it. And then attack the weakness with the power of the Lord and heaven's armies.

> Sometimes we need to feel the *pain*. We need to feel the reality of the struggle. Because that's where God can help.

God knows, God sees, and God cares so, so much. Because of who he is. And because of who we are.

It hit me in church that morning. Okay, so our pastor recited a scripture that blasted me into where I needed to be.

"Then he said to her, 'Daughter, your faith has healed you. Go in peace.'" (Luke 8:48)

I heard *Daughter*.
I heard *faith. Healed*. And *peace*.

Who Are You?

I am his. And so are you. Daughter. Son. Child of God. Chosen. Of the King. On the highest throne. Over all things. You are heir of the Almighty. The Perfect. The Creator. The King of the kingdom, the infinite universe, everything. You and me. And we are his. Princess. Prince. Beloved. Cherished. Protected. By the good sovereign God.

Now here I soar above the clouds. Held, loved. Clinging to my faith. Healed of the chains of fear. Not because my fear has completely vanished. But because I fly despite the fear. Because as I hold on to my Father's hand for dear life, he sustains me, lifts me, and lends me touches of peace. Like a sponge with a million holes and empty gaps, I drench myself in his presence, soak in his radiance, and let him fill the hollow of all that is hard.

Do you know who *you* are?

When along your path to overcome worry, nothing seems to work. Or you find what once worked, stops. Remember who you are. You are the most cherished treasure in your Father's house. And he is a good, good Father. I don't know what you've heard, or what you've come to think that reflects otherwise, but it's a guaranteed promise. He cares for you. He will care for you. He will protect you. Always. You are his. And so am I.

> **You are the most cherished treasure in your Father's house. And he is a good, good Father.**

I am so thankful. Daughter of the King. These are the words singing through my soul as the clouds carry me. What a gift that I have taken for granted.

I am resting in gratitude. And find thankfulness for this moment. Moments when all we have, all I have, all I need, is him. To be cradled, most intimately, 100 percent dependent. On him. Alone. I let him permeate my being and fuel fast on the speck of peace in the calm. In the smoother moments. Breathing deeply here. You never know how long it will last, but when God gives you sweet, serene seconds or minutes, feel them, and fill up on them.

The captain interrupts over the intercom, "In about seven to ten minutes it's going to get pretty bumpy."

I put down my pen, close my eyes, and rest in God's arms.

Then through the clouds. I take a peek. No sight of sky above or earth below. Just dense clouds.

God is here.

He carried me here. He never lets go.

And suddenly, I can see again. The world below closer and closer, coming into focus. Perfectly plotted streets, highways, and waterways. Power lines, swimming pools, ponds. Then chimneys, streetlights, and satellite dishes. And a safe landing.

God was there. He had my hand, all of me, the whole way. And I held him tight.

Blessing of Brokenness

When you take God with you through your brokenness and fear, you encounter him in the sweetest spiritual, most intimate way. It's divinely beautiful. It infuses the pit of fear, carries you through with peace and joy, as your eyes are fixed on him and your heavenly home.

Despite the struggle, I am so thankful for these dear encounters. And if my fear never completely disappears, I can still be thankful and rejoice for the privilege of connecting so deeply with my Father. The greatest lover my soul will ever know.

> When you take God with you through your brokenness and fear, you encounter him in the sweetest spiritual, most intimate way.

I know your fears and worries may be your worst enemy. They can drive you positively ballistic and you want them gone for good. But if the struggle sticks around a while longer, know that God may very well allow this—every weakness that you wear, for that matter—to bless you with the opportunity to enjoy sweet communion with the filling essence of who he is. A chance to see his power, to experience his nearness and compassionate love. To experience vulnerable dependence on him, his strength, growth, endurance, and faithfulness. And the gift of shining his light on those you encounter through your attentive enrichment.

Gift of Grace

But here's another constant battle for many of us. Or me anyway. What if I slip up and neglect to be so diligent in my efforts to lock arms with God through the storms of my struggles? Will he still show up when fear sneaks up on me and I don't have the luxury of preparing for the blow? Or just plain forget? Or when I numb out with a worldly resolution? Sadly, I slowly realized, deep down, I wasn't so sure I was worthy if my godly striving was subpar.

Have you ever felt like you aren't worthy of God's protection? As if maybe you haven't been good enough to deserve the good promises laid out in his faithful Word?

I totally have.

In the weeks leading up to my big flight, I ensured I was checking all the boxes. Extra prayer time, check. Double doses of Scripture reading, got it. Loving others harder, practicing patience, watching the words that fly out of my mouth, along with the food, fuel, and nutrition that fly in—covered. And when I finally arrived safely to my vacation destination, I tanked. Flat-out exhausted.

Next up, I prayed a little prayer here, thanked God for the gorgeous emerald ocean there. But not so sure I'd match my prior attempts or get an A+ for scriptural diligence and modeling the life of a holy roller while beach-bumming it.

And then by my final morning preparing for the flight home, my nerves were screaming at me all over again. *All I want to do is make it home safe, kiss the ground of my hometown, the foreheads of all five of my missed-and-loved-like-crazy kids! And I'm not sure I'm deserving and worthy!*

But something hard-core struck me in my brief quiet time with God the dawn of that last day. Something I'd heard enough times that my stubborn soul should know better, but that I'd never fully grasped in my time knowing Jesus.

It doesn't matter.

My protection, my identity, the seal of unconditional love wrapped snug around my whole being, came with an "as is" guarantee. My performance doesn't change a thing. My striving won't make me any more loved, or any more protected, cared for, or watched over. It's a free gift. The greatest gift.

> My protection, my identity, the seal of unconditional love wrapped snug around my whole being, came with an "as is" guarantee.

Absolutely, God is overjoyed when we give him back the gift of our time and attention, and we will enjoy many more of his peaceful, joyful blessings when we embrace him. But nothing you do, or don't do, will change the amount of care he gives you. How much freedom and rest is there in that? Truth be told, we can wear ourselves out trying to check all the good Samaritan boxes. But more than anything, God just wants you to know you are unconditionally claimed and loved as his child.

My flight home was leaps and bounds better. I took notes of the reminders and my conviction of his great mercy and grace when the flight first lifted off. But then I closed my notebook, allowed God to hold me up when the wafts of worry whipped through me, and rested a little more in the truth that he had me no matter what. I rested in profound trust.

I had been peeling off, layer by sticky layer, the worrier label. And now here I rested, unleashing the final fold, revealing the sparkle of my true God-made self.

Wearing Your God-Given Identity

What would it look like for you to remove your old worrier label and permanently adopt and apply your God-ordained "Warrior of Trust" identity as the child of God you were born into? I mean, what does it truly look like to steadfastly wear your authentic identity and rightful armor of God?

It's no secret now that I love the *Jesus Calling* devotionals. And am amazed over and over how God uses these devotional words at the most impeccably perfect moments. In fact, I had previously made note of that day's focus verse, Ephesians 6:16, on my very first flight from Louisville to our Atlanta layover.

> In addition to all this, take up the shield of faith, with which you can extinguish all the flaming arrows of the evil one. (Eph. 6:16)

Now here I sat, heart changed, reopening my personal journal, laying hands over these relevant words in Ephesians. Eyes closed, ears tuned to Carrie Underwood's *My Savior* album, I humbly meditated on this verse. Yes, Lord. I will. Yes, I need your shield so desperately to help me fight. I will take it up and arm myself from fear. From the evil one.

And then, with the Holy Spirit, my mind drifted. To Peter walking on water. Taking up the shield looks like Peter walking on water. I opened my Bible. Peering into the Gospel, picking up my pencil, I wrote down every word from that story in Matthew 14, and let it speak over me.

I was captivated by the moment this follower of Jesus, fueled by his faith, stepped out onto the water, became frightened with doubt as the wind picked up, but then cried out to the Lord to save him. And two significant things struck me: Peter cried out, and Jesus *immediately* caught him. And this was me in that moment: the cry and the catch.

We pick up our shield of faith when we cry out to God in fear. And he catches us. He may not necessarily keep you from sinking below the surface of actual water in the literal sense, if you take a plunge without a life vest. But when doubt, anxiousness, and trembling fear start to take their weary toll on you, call on him, go to him, arm up with him. He will catch you with the peace of his presence, the caress of his love, a shot of his strength, or a jolt of his joy. This is huge news. It is for me anyway. He will not let me fall. He will catch you too.

> We pick up our shield of faith when we cry out to God in fear. And he catches us.

Then I pondered a little deeper on what it looks like to permanently wear this armor of God. When fear, anxiety, and worry triggers confront you, it looks like, not just arming when the wind picks up, but taking up the shield of faith each and every day. When the wind is calm or war is raging. Sometimes every single breath of a moment. Yes, holding up this shield, boldly wearing the badge of a God-trusting warrior, is a continual choice and a continual battle.

It looks like strapping on the complete and full armor of God described in Ephesians 6.

Finally, be strong in the Lord and in his mighty power. Put on the full armor of God, so that you can take your stand against the devil's schemes. For our struggle is not against flesh and blood, but against the rulers, against the authorities, against the powers of this dark world and against the spiritual forces of evil in the heavenly realms. Therefore put on the full armor of God, so that when the day of evil comes, you may be able to stand your ground, and after you have done everything, to stand. Stand firm then, with the belt of truth buckled around your waist, with the breastplate of righteousness in place, and with your feet fitted with the readiness that comes from the gospel of peace. In addition to all this, take up the shield of faith, with which you can extinguish all the flaming arrows of the evil one. Take the helmet of salvation and the sword of the Spirit, which is the word of God. (Eph. 6:10–17)

It looks like being strong in the Lord, facing the enemy of fear, loading up with every faith-filled tool you've learned so you can stand firm in truth, righteousness, and peace. And holding tight to the shield that will resist the evil one. Clinging to your salvation, the Spirit, and the unshakable Word of God. Over and over and over again.

Christ in You

You have a choice. You can choose the bulletproof armor of God. And you should. We all should. Choose to be more than blessed. He promises to catch you, save you, protect you, with peace and power. You can fight the relentless lies of the enemy. You can battle back against worry, and fear, and anxious thoughts. And not just with the tools beside you, but with Christ in you.

> You can fight the relentless lies of the enemy. You can battle back against worry, and fear, and anxious thoughts. And not just with the tools beside you, but with Christ in you.

When Christ died for you and for me, he became available to all who believe. Believer, you have the spirit of Christ with you *and* in you. Accepting your identity in Christ is a continual choice. To continually walk in the trusted truths we have practiced, and in the belief system we are staking our claim in, we must choose to fight the lies of the liar constantly. We must adopt a new, nonstop, relentless lifestyle of moving closer to living in the truth, with persistent perseverance.

If you haven't fully accepted Christ as the living God, the one who can set you free from the chains of the enemy, the one who gave his life to give you yours, or if you need to recommit your heart to standing firm in this, I pray you will. The best life lies in laying yours down in this truth. His truth. And if it's the truth you struggle with, I would like to encourage you to seek out a mentor of doctrinal knowledge or grab a reliable book about the life and truths of our Savior, the Messiah.

God is in us. Christ, in us. The Spirit, in us. As a believer, the Savior of the world is in you. How wonderful.

Take Flight

So, what now?

For me, I will fly again. I will continue to face my fears, with him and for him. I will keep running into the storms of life the Lord leads me to. Knowing he will lead me through. I want to keep growing, conquering, acknowledging God's presence with me. Leaning closer and closer, learning deeper and deeper his perfect, protecting love that casts out all fear.

> I will keep running into the storms of life the Lord leads me to. Knowing he will lead me through.

While remnants of worry might linger and may continue on this side of heaven, I can still rejoice. With thankfulness for the gift from God of the most intimate moments when all I have is him. To be cradled in my weakness, in my brokenness, in my fear. And in his mighty good, tender loving hands. Cradled in peace, through to an abundance of purpose and joy.

I can only imagine where life might take me with the confident ability to continue taking on my fear. Maybe Israel. To walk where Jesus walked. Stand where he stood, pray where he prayed, experience the fullness of life where he loved, lived, and changed the world. Maybe I'll venture across the country to see my niece marry the love of her life. To the beautiful West Coast that only the eyes of my mind have seen. Or the romantic countryside of Italy, or Greece, or Hawaii, Alaska, or Bora Bora. Oh, I could only hope. It all sounds so lovely to me.

How about you? What might life to the full look like on the other side of your fear? Where would you travel, what would you see, what would you do, who would you meet? Would you work a little less and experience more time with people? Would you change jobs and find more profound purpose? Would you move to a new town and explore the blessing of learning a new way of life for your family? Go back to school? Sign up for a singles' group, single folks? Encourage your kids to try new things or follow their passions? What new things would you try? What things would you let go of if you let go of worry?

What fears still simmer inside that you need to face with God and find the immeasurable blessings he has waiting for you to unwrap, to unleash more wonder and fullness in this one life you have to live? There's a beautiful world out there waiting for you. God created it for you.

Friend, it's time to take flight away from fear and into freedom. I pray you will take flight with me into a new chapter of life. A bold life of following the Lord, who is calling you closer. A good God who has good, grand plans for you. A God who loves you insanely, beautifully, enormously, beyond your wildest dreams. The God over all creation. The King of your heart. A God you can trust. Who will meet you in the midst of all your fears. Capable of all things. Everything.

Take flight with me into a new life of greater kinship with the good sovereign Father, will you?

Who are you?

You are a blessed, beloved child . . . of the Most High.

Of the Almighty King. Holy Spirit, Christ alive in you. Beside you. Holding you forevermore.

And so, you have nothing to worry about. Nothing to fear.

Fly and soar with him.

And keep soaring. Keep seeking and listening. Keep walking bold as ever in obedience hand in hand with him. All the way through your purpose-filled life ahead, to your home in heaven. Standing firm in who you are and whose you are.

Remember what we've learned. To pray more, release control, believe the truth of God's unconditional love and perfect power. Practice peace, thankfulness and joy, obedience and purpose. And again, always remember who you are.

You were not born a worrier. Even though you may have a DNA spiked with anxiety, life has had its way with you, and the world has tried to convince you otherwise. It's time to shake off these old labels. You were purposefully tailor-made and breathed into this world a *warrior*. Because you have God in you and for you. Made in his holy image. The absolute victor over all. With all the armor to fight the enemy of worry and fear. To battle and conquer the lies of the deceiver.

> You were not born a worrier. You were purposefully tailor-made and breathed into this world a *warrior*. Because you have God in you and for you.

For everyone born of God overcomes the world. This is the victory that has overcome the world, even our faith.
(1 John 5:4)

You are a God-trusting warrior with the power to overcome the evil worries of the world. Even when the sting of the struggle persists, even when the pain prompts you to avoid the storm, wear that warrior label. And walk into who you are, who you were meant to be. In and through him.

God is calling . . .

You are worthy. *Always.*

You are not helpless. *Always.*

You can win over worry and soar with the One who overcomes because you have him.

Always.

REFLECTION QUESTIONS

1. Have you made progress with your win over worry? What triggers can you be aware of to prepare you for your future fight with fear?

2. Describe your true identity in God. Do you know you are sealed with his love and protection not because of what you do, but because of who he is? Explain.

3. What worries do you still need to let go of and let God get closer to? What's holding you back?

4. Are you ready to take flight into a new chapter of life as a *God-trusting warrior*? How and what will that look like?

Finish with a prayer of gratitude to the Overcomer, and a commitment to choose him, to help you continue to win over worry.

ACKNOWLEDGMENTS

"Where would I be without you? Where would I be, Jesus?"
These lyrics from Zach Williams—yes! 100 percent. Amen.
The words on these pages. The struggle and redemption of these
stories. The renewal, revival, and rescue. All because of you, Lord
Jesus. And all *for* you. May I spend every last day you bless me
with breath worshiping you for bringing life to what once was lost.
Thank you for drawing me in with each passing year of your love
and lessons. You never stopped knocking, you were constantly
there, and your plan was in motion before I could even fathom
such a perfect purpose. You were crafting and continue to com-
pose a story with my life that you intended to share for your glory.
How beautiful. You planted the passion and lent me the strength
to say yes. God, you alone made all this possible. I stand in awe.
Your grace upon grace has been endless, unique, and personal.
You brought me your people for this assignment. And I praise you.

You brought me my husband. You knew what I needed more
than I did. A man who would support with all his heart a calling

you would slowly reveal to me. To writing, to full-time ministry, to an opening of my hands to wherever you might lead.

So to Michael, my love, thank you for your unwavering encouragement. For your ceaseless care of the balls I dropped in getting these words into a thirsty-for-living-water world. For your pick-me-ups when I felt like a failure. For your patience when I couldn't see the light. For the walks and long talks. The hugs, love, and escape dates to tear me away from the grip of the enemy's attempts to consume me. Thank you, one thousand times forever.

Will, Abigail, Kaitlyn, Mallory, and Hannah Kate. How could I possibly deserve you? You don't even know the sacrifice you've made for your mom. The snuggles I could've given, the extra counsel I could've offered, the attention instead of weariness, patience instead of frustration, while fixating on the task before me. But God—he provided for you. And for me. He assured that in my pursuit of obedience he would care for you. For all things. Through you he reflected his love, grace, and promises. Will, your love for the Lord. Abigail, your shining spirit-filled soul. Kaitlyn, your delightful tender heart. Mallory, your infectious zest for life. And Hannah Kate, your constant, compassionate embrace. Each of you is a gift from above. I have never been so thankful, and I love all five of you more than words can speak.

Mom and Dad. You just might be my biggest fans. From day one you've been there. Molding, modeling, loving like Christ. This is *everything*. My love for you is immeasurable. My sister, Amy. You know my stories well, walked many of them with me, and I cherish you and your support. John, you love so big and make me beyond proud to call you brother. You mean the world to me. My servant-hearted in-laws, who offered helping hands and hearts to make more space for this creation. I am so thankful. My dear J times eight plus C clan (John, Jennifer, Jill, Janie, Josie, Jake, Josh,

J.J., and Cassie), loads of awesome aunts, uncles, and cousins. I have one fine family behind me. Bless you!

Church family, and especially my Bible study girls. You're simply amazing! There is a wealth of you but each so uniquely significant you call for your own shout out. Allison, I love you like a sister. *Muah!* Jamie, your faith and friendship have touched my life. Same for you, Dawn, Elizabeth, Michelle, Monique, Susan, Becky, Ellen, Emily, and Emily. We are without a doubt having a sweet blast growing and doing life together. I cherish you and raise a glass to sharing blessings to come! Victoria, Sara, Ellen, Ashlea, Lisa, Sue, Becky, and Cheryl, you're my prayer warriors, my relentless encouragers, and I'm truly better because of each of you. And then there's Amanda, Devin, Shelly, Christina, Jenny, Amie, and Ronda. You didn't even know it, but the love of Christ that flows through you left sweet impressions through this mission as well.

Dear friends. Every hard-fought success has one heck of a cheerleading squad. A team of heaven's earth angels. Rachael, God orchestrated our divine meeting, and our Christian sisterhood has not only been invaluable but also pivotal in my journey—a solid rock of the Lord. Melissa, I'm beyond blessed by your wisdom and godly friendship. Where in the world have you been all my life!? Sarah and Jessica, you are long-time friends who continue to hold a dear place in my heart, and you certainly made your mark on this message. Melissa, Julie, Tonya, and Scott, your love left an imprint as well. Thank you.

To Kyle Idleman, my senior pastor, God has you hard at task, yet you humbly prayed over this work and backed the message when it was just being shaped. I thank the good Lord for your encouragement, endorsement, and blessing. And to the rest of my endorsers, Wendy Pope, Carol McLeod, Rachael Adams, Lisa Appelo, Ashley Morgan Jackson, Rebecca George, and Sarah Geringer, a gigantic THANK YOU. You sacrificially invested in me and took a chance on a new author. What an absolute gift your affirmation and support has been. Truly.

Speaking of taking a chance. My agent, Blythe Daniel, and Leafwood Publishers. I prayed much longer than I wanted for the most suitable champions of this book, and God led me to a perfect pair who turned my message into his masterpiece. I know it will be divinely used to serve and redeem many. How grateful I am for you!

I would be remiss if I didn't express the remarkable impression of the few who proudly cheered on my calling initially but now celebrate this release side-by-side with Jesus. My precious "Papa" and "Dodie" (Ray and Donna Stoess). Your unconditional out-loud love always fueled my confidence to do anything. And my beloved brother-in-law, James. You had a kindred craving to publish and now have the gift of living out your greatest dreams in heaven. I will forever treasure each of you.

I hesitated to list individuals because there were surely more people God purposefully placed behind the scenes to pattern the success of this book. My launch team, social media friends, friends of friends. Strangers to me that haven't been brought into my life and mind yet. I pray I have the pleasure to thank you soon enough.

And to you, reading these words. God hand selected each of you. I am wowed. Thank you, God, and thank *you*. For picking up my debut book, hanging with me, and definitely for making it all the way through to my final thoughts. You are a gem of a soul. One I would be honored to become better acquainted with. So, can we connect some more? I hang out on Facebook and Instagram (probably more than I should—being honest), but mostly I just love to bond with and make new Jesus-lovin' friends!

And one last time. Bless you, bless you, bless you. Every single one of you. From the bottom of my grateful heart.

REFERENCES

Allen, Jennie. *Get Out of Your Head: Stopping the Spiral of Toxic Thoughts.* Colorado Springs: Waterbrook, 2020.

Beck, Judith S. *Cognitive Therapy: Basics and Beyond.* New York: Guilford, 1995.

———. *Cognitive Therapy for Challenging Problems: What to Do When the Basics Don't Work.* New York: Guilford, 2005.

Brown, Kane. "What Ifs." RCA Records Nashville, 2017.

Emmons, Henry. *The Chemistry of Calm: A Powerful, Drug-Free Plan to Quiet Your Fears and Overcome Your Anxiety.* New York: Touchstone, 2010.

Fuller, Malinda. *Obedience over Hustle: The Surrender of the Striving Heart.* Uhrichsville, OH: Shiloh Run, 2019.

MayoClinic.org. "Panic attacks and panic disorder." Accessed November 22, 2022. https://www.mayoclinic.org/diseases-conditions/panic-attacks/symptoms-causes/syc-20376021.

Meyer, Joyce. *Unshakeable Trust: Find the Joy of Trusting God at All Times, in All Things.* New York: Faith Words, 2017.

Perry, Maggie. "Redirect Rumination." *Huddle.care Weekly.* October 20, 2019. https://huddlecareweekly.substack.com/.

Pote, Allen. "Psalm 139." Chorister's Guild, 1992.

TerKeurst, Lysa. *The Best Yes: Making Wise Decisions in the Midst of Endless Demands.* Nashville: Thomas Nelson, 2014.

———. *What Happens When Women Walk in Faith: Trusting God Takes You to Amazing Places.* Eugene, OR: Harvest House, 2005.

Voskamp, Ann. *One Thousand Gifts: A Dare to Live Fully Right Where You Are.* Nashville: Thomas Nelson, 2011.

Williams, Zach. "Rescue Story." *Rescue Story.* Provident Label Group, 2019.

Worthington, Alli. *Fierce Faith: A Woman's Guide to Fighting Fear, Wrestling Worry, and Overcoming Anxiety.* Grand Rapids: Zondervan, 2018.

Young, Sarah. *Jesus Calling: 365 Devotions with Real-Life Stories.* Nashville: Thomas Nelson, 2019.